MAKING NEWS

The Ultimate Guide to Handling the Media

CHRIS URQUHART

Copyright © 2021 Chris Urquhart

Published by Immediate Communications

All rights reserved. No part of this publication may be reproduced, transmitted or distributed in any manner whatsoever without the prior written permission of the publisher.

The information contained within this book is for general use purposes only. The author and publisher disclaim any liability in connection with the use of this information.

Interior Design: © Immediate Communications
Cover Imagery: © Can Stock Photo / IvicaNS /Abscent / Immediate Communications

ISBN: 978-0-6452152-0-5

For Dad, who taught me confidence.
For Mum, who showed me resilience.

For Liz, who brings me love and laughter.
And for Zachary, who gives everything purpose.

Thank you.

CONTENTS

Introduction — 1

PART I. MEDIA TRAINING: WHAT YOU NEED TO KNOW

1. Australia's Changing Media — 7
2. Why Should I Give An Interview? — 15
3. Dealing With Reporters — 25
4. Prep Step One: Ask Some Questions — 37
5. Prep Step Two: Set a Goal — 47
6. Prep Step Three: Choose Key Messages — 51
7. Prep Step Four: Make it Memorable — 59
8. Prep Step Five: Practice — 71
9. The Prep Steps In Action: A Case Study — 75

10.	The Different Interviews You'll Face	81
11.	Handling Tough Questions	109
12.	More Than Words	127
13.	Creating Calm and Dealing With Nerves	145
14.	Questions I Always Get Asked	153

PART II. MEDIA TRAINING: WHAT THEY SHOULD HAVE KNOWN

15. Real World Media Training Lessons — 167
    Aussie politicians and dangerous backdrops — 167
    The empty chair at ABC's 7.30 — 169
    Barack Obama's chit-chat — 170
    Caught off guard by a boom microphone — 171
    Upsetting the Wolf of Wall Street — 173
    Ronald Reagan's dangerous sarcasm — 174
    An Aussie politician forgets his messages — 175
    Nick Kyrgios' unique interview style — 176
    What happened to Kourtney? — 177
    Prince Andrew's right royal mess — 179
    Big oil boss makes a big mistake — 180
    A motoring enthusiast joins the Senate — 181
    John Hewson's birthday cake — 182
    Rolls Royce CEO — 184
    Supermarket boss sings "We're in the Money" — 185

    Chris Urquhart's "Edge" Training Courses — 187
    About Chris Urquhart — 191

INTRODUCTION

My life in the media

I was a reporter and presenter on radio and television for about fifteen years. It was a wild adventure that took me around Australia and around the world, covering all manner of stories, great and small. Over the years, I interviewed hundreds of politicians, CEOs, sports stars and entertainers. My work took me from the press gallery in Canberra, to the front line of terrorism at the Lindt Café in Sydney. One day, I'd be raiding drug dens with a police SWAT team in Miami, on another, chasing crocodiles with the Irwin family in remote North Queensland. From red carpet interviews, to the red dust of droughts, and the red flames of bushfires. Such were the dizzying highs and devastating lows of a career in the media. I'm so grateful for everything it taught me about our world, and for what it taught me about the people in it.

Above all, I learnt the power of storytelling. Stories have connected us since the dawn of time. Our oldest ancestors would sit around a fire at night, sharing stories of their journeys and adventures. They'd leave their marks in artwork on caves, for future generations to discover their stories too. Later, stories were etched on to stone tablets or papyrus. Then centuries later, the printing press would mean stories could be shared further and more widely than ever before. Later, radio, television and the internet meant stories could be shared around the world in an instant. The methods of sharing stories might have changed, but the power of them never has.

One of the most valuable skills any of us can have is the ability to tell our own story. And one of the most efficient ways to share our story with millions of people at once, is through an interview with a journalist from the media.

In my time as a journalist, I'd often speak to business leaders, spokespeople and others who were incredibly talented in their field, and who had achieved great success, but couldn't quite understand how to get their story or message across. Many of them were terrified to interact with a journalist and weren't sure what to say and what to do. At best, they'd fluke their way through. At worst, their interviews were disastrous, damaging to their own reputation and the organisations they were representing.

It was a shame, because so many benefits can come from a good media interview. Communicating effectively and concisely isn't a skill that comes naturally to everyone, but it is certainly one that can be learnt.

Leaders who take time to learn the art of communication and storytelling, and gain the skills to give a successful media interview, are well-placed to promote their organisation in good times, and are in a much stronger position to defend it during a crisis. With so much at stake, communications and media training isn't a luxury for leaders, it is an absolute necessity.

When I decided that my journalism career had taken me on enough adventures, I knew that I wanted to go from telling stories myself, to empowering other people to tell their own.

In the years since, I've trained hundreds of business leaders, politicians, emergency services personnel, sportspeople, entertainers and entrepreneurs in the art of effective communication, message delivery and how to handle themselves in media interviews. In the many training sessions I have conducted, I've shared secrets on how to prepare, how to remain calm, how to deal with nerves and how to handle difficult questions when they arise. Most of all I explain the power of a story, and the importance of being able to share it.

What I share in training sessions and in this book is based on everything I learnt in a long career at programs like Nine News, Seven News, A Current Affair, Today and the ABC's 7.30. I'm good at helping people answer tough questions because I'm so used to asking them.

That's my story. And this book is all about helping you tell yours.

Chris Urquhart

PART I

MEDIA TRAINING: WHAT YOU NEED TO KNOW

1.

AUSTRALIA'S CHANGING MEDIA

What happened to the news?

The media in Australia is undergoing an overwhelming period of change.

Not so long ago, Australians relied on just a handful of news sources to find out about the world around them. We might have read a newspaper in the morning, listened to the radio on the drive to work and watched the six o'clock news on the television at night. Perhaps before bed, we'd have flicked through a magazine, too.

In the twentieth century, the news media was among the most profitable of industries. Some of Australia's wealthiest families — the Packer, Murdoch and Fairfax dynasties — made their fortunes building vast media empires in publishing and broadcasting.

Then the internet changed everything. Suddenly, we had more sources to choose from and there was more competition for our limited attention spans. No longer were readers and viewers limited to the newspaper or television station in their local town. Suddenly we could get our news from anywhere in the world, at any time.

Until the age of the internet, one reason media owners became wealthy was that they owned the relatively limited means of production in their field. There were only a handful of broadcasting licences and they were expensive. The infrastructure of printing presses and the logistics of distribution meant newspaper proprietors faced little competition.

But with the internet, suddenly anyone could become a publisher by starting their own website. Some people launched blogs, which grew into digital media empires, such as Mia Freedman's Mamamia. Around the world, new outlets like Vice and BuzzFeed competed for readers with household names and traditional titles like The New York Times and The Sydney Morning Herald. What it all meant was that audiences, once concentrated in the hands of a few programs or newspapers, became fragmented as the public's attention was diverted to new entrants to the market.

Even before the internet though, the advent of cable television, and with it, 24-hour news channels, brought an upheaval to the news cycle. News become instant, and constant. The 24-hour news cycle quickly became a 24-second news cycle, as deadlines were obliterated and news events and opinions were broadcast in real-time around the clock. The immediacy of this type of broadcasting meant fact-checking was frequently overlooked in the race to be first with a story. Nuance and context also started to take a back seat. Because of the relentless demand from journalists, organisations facing a crisis had to learn to respond to the media straight away. They no longer had the luxury of time to craft their responses.

The next stage of the evolution was the rise of smartphones and social media. People could now catch up with news headlines before they were even out of bed in the morning, and be updated regularly through push notifications or their social media feeds throughout the day. They could share the stories they were reading with friends on their own social media accounts. Information spread easily. Unfortunately, misinformation did too.

As audiences fragmented and divided across multiple news sources, advertising money was spread more thinly and revenue and profits declined. The consequence we are now experiencing is that many publications and programs are, nowadays, staffed by fewer journalists. The reporters who remain are much busier and required to do a lot more.

Once upon a time, a reporter might have all day to work up a story for a newspaper. These days, that same reporter might file several stories, update them online, record their own videos, take their own photographs, and do phone interviews with radio stations too. That's in between posting on their social media accounts to share the story, and planning for a podcast they might be appearing on later in the week.

Reporters are busy. And for busy reporters, interviewees who make their lives easier by understanding the requirements of an interview and what makes a good story, are a welcome relief. Media training has never been more important.

The media isn't dead

Despite all of these changes, reports of the death of the media, to twist Mark Twain's words a little, have been greatly exaggerated. The media has evolved. It's changed. It's adapted. It's mutated. And it's gone digital. But it isn't dead, even in traditional formats. Far from it.

When it comes to television news, the major Australian commercial bulletins still attract a combined audience in the millions every evening. In addition to these flagship broadcasts, there's also early morning news, mid-morning news, afternoon news and evening bulletins too. Add the ABC, 24-hour channels, breakfast variety programs and investigative shows and the result is a lot of news content still on TV, being watched by a lot of people.

As for radio, many millions of people still tune in to their favourite radio entertainment, music and talkback stations each week. Is it dead? No. Has it changed? Sure. These days, more programs are syndicated across multiple cities and regional areas don't have as much local programming as they once did, but radio in Australia still has an enormous audience and a big impact. Many radio stations have modernised their approaches, becoming key players in the hyper-competitive podcast market.

Newspapers, though declining in circulation, are still being published and some of the biggest scoops still appear in print first. Millions still read our newspapers, and many millions more turn to online sites for their news fix. As an example, around 10 million people log on to news.com.au, one of Australia's most popular online news sites, every month. And that's just one of countless news websites, blogs, industry and trade publications that boast impressive and growing online audiences.

In all formats, both traditional and modern, people are consuming media in enormous numbers. These huge audiences are an obvious reason to take your organisation's media profile seriously, both by seeking out positive opportunities and preparing to defend your reputation in times of crisis.

Big opportunities, big risks

These new digital destinations and their audiences present fresh opportunities for organisations seeking publicity. Websites and 24-hour news channels need constantly updated content and new stories. There is a vacuum of airtime, column space and internet pages to fill and journalists want to interview spokespeople, so that they can create stories to fill these voids. Journalists want visual opportunities that will keep viewers watching on TV and engaged and clicking on their stories online.

There has never been more opportunity to get your story

out there, and these days, stories spread quickly online. Once one publication publishes a report, others will often follow with their own version, sometimes lifting quotes and information from the original, perhaps with little regard for the ethics of doing so.

If it's good news being reported about your organisation, that's fabulous for you! But if it's bad news? That can be disastrous. Going viral, so to speak, might be a blessing, or it could be a curse. The element of risk is another reason why becoming familiar with the media and understanding how modern journalists and newsrooms operate is so crucial. If you understand the way they work, you can confidently shape your organisation's message from the very beginning, and deal with the fallout if things spin out of control.

The arrival of social media

If the traditional media is tricky to negotiate, social media certainly is too. From the perspective of risk, social media provides a fresh new way that an organisation's reputation, built carefully over the years, can be damaged within minutes. Customers, for example, who once aired their grievances in private, now do so in public on social media pages for the entire world to see.

On social media, news travels fast. And citizen journalists have taken the news into their own hands. Everyone has a camera on their smartphone, and many are not afraid to use it — and then tweet or post what they've recorded. A customer's experience, an opinion, an image or a video gets shared, and soon it's all over the web. Social media has become a treasure trove of stories for journalists looking for a scoop.

Social media can fan the fire of a small story into an enormous blaze. Fast-paced news coverage means increasing demand for organisations to respond immediately to criticism. Being ready to engage with the media in all its new and different forms is more important than ever and being on the front foot is crucial.

But don't worry. The good news is social media brings plenty of positive opportunities too. Organisations can now publish and broadcast their own news to the dedicated audiences that they've built on their own social media channels. And pesky reporters aren't there to filter the news either, or ask hard questions. Businesses can create and share their own text, photos, videos and links. Got news to break? If you want, you can break it yourself, broadcasting live on Facebook, YouTube or other platforms. What's next? Smart businesses are also evolving their publishing and broadcasting beyond social media in formats such as podcasts, video content, and their own blogs and news websites.

A sensible approach, if you want to connect with the public, is to use a mix of both social and traditional forms of media. And whichever forms you engage with, the principles of good communication and clear messaging remain very much the same.

Why do media training?

Engaging with the media is a high-stakes game. Audience

numbers, whether traditional, digital or social, run into the many millions. If you are a strong, confident communicator whose interactions with the public via the media are good, you will enjoy the massive rewards. Your organisation will bathe in the positive publicity, your sales will grow, your reputation will increase and the sky is the limit. At a personal level, it can't hurt your own career either.

But if you misstep or misspeak, your mistakes can destroy both your organisation's reputation and your own, and ruin years of hard work. It can be humiliating. Engaging with the media comes with highs and lows, with risks and rewards. But the risks can be mitigated if you are adequately prepared.

Because dealing with journalists is uncharted territory for most, media training helps demystify the experience, and gives you the opportunity to build your confidence, become a clear communicator and enjoy all the rewards that come as a result of telling your own story.

2.

WHY SHOULD I GIVE AN INTERVIEW?

Because there's something you want to say

The main reason to participate in a media interview is because you have something to say. The reason to say it to a media outlet is that the size of their audience means you will be able to say it to an enormous group of people at once.

Communication, in any form, is all about sending a message and having it received and understood. If you send an SMS, the message might go to one person. If you tell a story at a dinner party, the message might go to a handful of people. If you speak at a conference, the message might go to a few hundred people. If you send an email to your customer list, the message might go to a few thousand people. But if you send a message via a media interview, it could well go to millions of people and travel around the globe.

So communicating via the media is really all about

efficiency. It's about reaching a large number of people in a short amount of time. As a spokesperson you have a message, and the media has the audience. When you give an interview, in a way you're just *using* the interviewer, in a transactional sense, to access their audience. The challenge is to make sure your message is interesting enough that a media outlet will want to share it with its audience. We'll discuss how to do that later in the book.

Because not speaking up is risky too

I mentioned earlier that engaging with the media is a high-stakes game. It comes with huge potential rewards, but substantial risk, if not handled well. With that in mind, why do it at all? Why take such a big risk? The answer is that refusing media interviews is a massive risk as well. Not taking part in a story doesn't mean that a story will go away. Instead it means that others may speak on your behalf, criticise you or steal your organisation's spotlight. If you don't speak up on your own behalf, who will? Reporters often note in stories when businesses have refused to answer questions or respond. This evasiveness can cause additional damage to your reputation.

My view is that if you've received training, are adequately prepared and can see a clear benefit in participating, then it can be a very good idea to get involved and be interviewed. The right preparation can help you manage any risk.

Do you want the good news or the bad news?

Some of you will be reading this book because you are

seeking more publicity for your organisation and have a lot of good news to share with the public. Others will be reading because you know that at times there will be bad news about your organisation and you want to be able to handle the media when your business is being questioned by journalists for all the wrong reasons. The truth is that for businesses and the spokespeople who represent them, dealing with the media usually involves a little bit of both.

I try not to focus on "good news" or "bad news". Instead, I like to classify stories into two broad categories:

- Proactive stories, and
- Reactive stories

Proactive stories

Proactive stories are ones where your organisation has sought out media attention. They occur when you have something to say or announce and you want people to know about it. Your communications team or consultant will usually have alerted some journalists or issued a press release to let reporters know that a spokesperson is available for an interview.

A proactive story might be the launch of a new product, the announcement of an event or to share new government policies. We generally think of proactive stories as positive stories, or good news. Obviously it would be pretty unusual for a business to proactively seek bad news coverage for itself!

Proactive media opportunities are great because you usually

have plenty of time to prepare for them. Often these stories are in the pipeline for weeks or months in advance, meaning you will have the luxury of time to work on your messages, and plenty of opportunity for rehearsal interviews.

It's important, though, to remember that proactive stories don't always mean soft or easy interviews. Depending on the topic, you can and will still face scrutiny from journalists. They can seek deeper information from you and once the interview has begun there's nothing to stop them from questioning you on issues or matters not related to the proactive story that you hoped they would cover. You should be aware of and ready for this. Part of engaging with the media is being prepared to handle anything that journalists throw at you. They won't always make your life difficult, but in those moments when they do, you need to be ready. Later in the book we discuss how to handle difficult questions.

Reactive stories

Reactive stories are usually the ones that you haven't gone to great lengths to publicise and often amount to bad news. They are stories where you must react to an incident or event and provide some commentary, explanation or perspective. Examples of reactive stories might be a safety recall of one of your products or a security incident in the workplace. They might involve court action, harassment claims or a plummeting share price.

Sometimes you might know or expect that a reactive story is coming and is likely to hit the press. You might be crossing your fingers that no journalist will be tipped off about it. At other times though, you might be blindsided when it makes the news.

Sometimes reactive stories are totally out of your control, such as natural disasters or the work of your competitors. But sometimes you or your employees might be at fault and you will need to take total responsibility for a situation. Sometimes reactive stories lead to a crisis, but not always. At times, reactive stories might not even be about your business specifically, but could require your reaction to something affecting another business or issue in your industry or the community. Commenting on these stories might even be a good opportunity for your business. It all depends on the story and context.

One of the biggest differences between proactive stories and reactive stories is the amount of time you have to prepare your response. For a proactive story, you may have weeks. In a reactive story, you may have only minutes. This is why it's worth doing media training ahead of time.

Is it true that any publicity is good publicity?

It's an old catchy slogan, often repeated, but I'm not sure that it's always the case. If you're leading a business that's in the middle of a crisis and in the media for all the wrong reasons, you'd probably say you'd prefer no publicity to an onslaught of the bad stuff! What I will say though, is that a crisis is an important opportunity to protect, preserve and grow your organisation's reputation. Often it's not the crisis itself that you will be judged on, but how you react and deal with it. If you do a good job, your reputation will grow. But a poorly handled crisis can leave a negative impression that you might never shake. Often the key to a successful response is involving yourself in the story at the earliest opportunity in order to mount your defence.

When should I say no?

Of course, there will be times when it is not appropriate to participate in interviews. If you have a good communications team or consultant, they will help you make a judgment about whether it is wise or unwise. A decision will usually be reached by asking a few questions, such as:

- Is there a message we want to get across?
- Is there a clear benefit in it for us?
- Are there risks in taking part?
- Will there be consequences if we don't participate?

Sometimes there will be perfectly good reasons for not agreeing to an interview. If there's a case before the courts, for example, there might be legal reasons not to do so. In the business world, there might be regulatory reasons that prevent a CEO from answering questions before a statement has been issued to the stock exchange. Sometimes you might just not want your brand associated with the angle of a particular story. Or perhaps the questions might deal with issues that are commercial-in-confidence. An experienced communications team or consultant will help you weigh the pros and cons of being interviewed for a story.

Even when you are very limited in what you can say, there may still be a way to shape the story by issuing a short statement or making brief comments. And later in the book, we will touch on the ways that you can still give an interview, using specific communications techniques to deal with questions that you are not in a position to answer. If you're adequately media trained and have confidence to get your message across, my view is you should seriously consider taking advantage of interview opportunities when they are offered. If you don't take the chance, your competitors might jump at the opportunity, or your detractors might speak on your behalf. And they're unlikely to be kind.

Get involved early

One of the most important pieces of advice I give organisations is that if they're going to be involved in a story, they ought to get involved at the earliest opportunity. Intervening and commenting early means that your organisation may be able to mitigate some damage by being on the front foot. It also means that other people who are interviewed after you for the story will have to respond to what you've said, rather than you responding to them.

Also, because there is so much replication, syndication, and sometimes outright plagiarism of stories across the web, if your comments appear in the original story, then they are likely to appear in re-written versions published elsewhere. This also means the opposite is true. If you hesitate or wait before speaking out, any replicated versions of the story won't include your commentary or point of view. If you want to have your say, you usually have to act quickly.

The other aspect of getting involved early is that reporters have deadlines and are working on a different timeline to your corporate machine. A reporter on deadline won't wait for you or your internal approval processes. Their story will be published or broadcast, with or without your involvement. So if they've given you a deadline, they mean it.

Always have a goal

I've always liked the old phrase "if you don't know where you're going, you'll never get there". It's useful in many instances in life, but especially when it comes to media interviews. There's a whole chapter dedicated to interview goal-setting later in this book, but I'm mentioning goal-setting a little earlier here, because it is perhaps the most important part of preparation. You absolutely must understand the essence of *why* you are giving a media interview. If you can crystallise *why* you are doing it, you'll be much better able to prepare and will give a much stronger interview.

What could the goal be?

Well, for a police officer, the goal of an interview might be: *"To get the public's help to find this missing person."*

For a pop star, the goal of an interview might be: *"I've got a new album, I'll be touring in November and I want people to buy tickets."*

For a politician, the goal of an interview might be: *"We want people to know that we have a new train timetable to make life easier for commuters (...oh, and we won't say this directly but we want to be re-elected!)"*

For a footballer who has behaved badly, the goal of an interview might be: *"I've let down the fans and I want them to know that I realise I've made a big mistake."*

For a CEO, the goal of an interview might be: *"I know shareholders are concerned about our revenue figures, but I want them to know we're on the road to recovery."*

Later in this book, we'll discuss a clear framework for preparing for any interview. At the core of the framework though, is having a goal and having key messages prepared to support you to achieve it. We'll discuss precisely how to do both later on, but I want to get you thinking about these concepts early in your media training journey.

Whose goal is it anyway?

Keep in mind, reporters will have a goal too and it might not match yours. By and large, their goal is to create a story that will interest and engage their audience. There are times when the reporter's goal and your goal will be the same. Take the example above, where police are searching for a missing person. Everyone from the police, to the family of the missing person, to the reporter and their media outlet are almost certainly united in a common goal: to locate the missing person and reunite their family.

But sometimes, your goal and the reporter's goal might be

at odds. The pop star mentioned above might have the goal of announcing a new album and tour. The reporter's goal though, might be to lure the pop star into a discussion about a rumoured love affair or poor ticket sales during their last tour.

It's entirely possible that even when your goal and the reporter's goal differ, a media interview might still lead to a worthwhile outcome for both of you. Take the CEO above, whose company's revenue has fallen. The reporter's goal might be a forensic look at the figures in the company's annual report. In their story, they might include information about the company's lower share price and revenue figures, but also include the quote from the CEO that she thinks the business is "on the road to recovery". The CEO might have preferred if the low revenue figures weren't reported, but by giving an interview, she at least had the opportunity to present her company's side of the story. We can chalk that up as a win for everyone. Or at the very least, the CEO has made the best of what could have been a bad situation.

3.

DEALING WITH REPORTERS

What are they really like?

Reporters come from all different walks of life, with different backgrounds and experiences. Some become specialists in a single field, while others are general reporters who cover a range of different topics and industries. In the past, journalists tended to start their career with a cadetship, often at a local or regional newspaper. These days, many young journalists have a university qualification. Like any segment of the population, reporters have a mix of interests, personalities, values and ethics.

Some surveys have placed trust in journalists at about the same level as trust in used car salespeople. Such comparisons are probably unfair to both decent, hardworking journalists, and decent, hardworking folks in car yards. After all, there are good and bad people in any occupation. It's true that some reporters are dishonest and will stop at nothing to get a story. Some prioritise sensationalism above all else. But my honest experience of many years in the industry is that those villains aren't in the majority.

After getting to know many hundreds of reporters over the years, my experience is that while there are exceptions, most reporters tend to share some common traits:

- Their priority is discovering and telling stories that will interest their audience.
- They know intimately the topics and issues that will engage their viewers, readers and listeners.
- They enjoy breaking down complicated subject matter so that everyday people can understand it.
- They know the parts of a story that will make their audience feel a certain way and place emphasis on these parts to attract and keep the audience's attention.
- They strive to be accurate and fair.
- They have pretty good BS detectors and can tell when someone is having them on.
- Where possible, they want to be first with exclusive stories or details that no other reporter has.
- Some can have an inflated sense of their own importance, possibly because they know that so many people are listening to what they say and reading what they write.
- They want to impress their boss so they can get a promotion, a pay-rise, a better job, a posting to an

overseas bureau or elevation to amore prestigious program or masthead.

There are plenty of exceptions to the traits above and some reporters will tick some of the boxes but not all of them. But if you want a sweeping generalisation, the list above is probably it.

However, a sweeping critique of reporters won't at all help you improve how you handle an interview. Nor will putting every journalist from a particular publication or broadcaster in the same category. It's a fact that some publications and broadcasters attract criticism because of their perceived political biases or questions over their ethics. But these organisations are usually large, employing reporters covering a range of different rounds. A sports reporter can't be held responsible for a salacious headline on their paper's front page, for example, and a finance reporter has no control over the opinions of the music reviewer!

I dislike the use of terms "the media" or "the mainstream media", when used as pejorative catch-alls to describe such a vast and diverse industry. The media is made up of so many different publications, and within these publications, so many different people. An idea of a vast conspiracy of journalists or media organisations is ridiculous. Every reporter, every interviewer and every media organisation you deal with will be a little different and have their own unique quirks and history of experience. Some will have been reporters for years, with decades of scoops under their belt. Others might still be at university, working part time on the job, while still completing their studies. A journalist's age or experience is not necessarily a guide to how thoroughly they will interview you, how well they know the topic, or how tough they will be.

Specialist reporters and interviewers

Some reporters will be specialists in their field. Large media organisations such as the ABC, metropolitan daily newspapers and commercial television networks have specialists in a range of reporting areas such as science, health, transport, sport, entertainment, Indigenous affairs, business, finance, economics, law and more.

These days there probably aren't as many specialist reporters or "roundspeople", who cover a "beat" as there used to be. As newsrooms shrink in size, the luxury of having a single reporter to cover one topic has become untenable for many publications. But that's not true everywhere.

Where they still exist, often these reporters will have covered the topic area for many years. They will have a strong grasp of the issues and context surrounding the particular industry they are covering. Their interviews might be a little tougher or call for more incisive detail because they know their audience will want it.

Away from mainstream media titles and programs, there are a lot of niche specialist reporters at websites and blogs. Car websites have specialist automotive reporters who know manufacturers and models from back to front. Finance websites may have experts with years of experience in the markets. Knowing that you are dealing with a specialist reporter or a specialist publication will frame your preparation for the interview.

General reporters and interviewers

For most of my reporting career, I was a general reporter. In both TV and radio, I quite liked the variety of covering different stories and different industries on different days. On one day, I was covering a building fire, the next day the launch of a new iPhone. Later that week I might cover a court case, and another day the opening of a motorway. For each of those stories, I had to very quickly get to know the subject matter. Perhaps I wasn't always able to conduct a deeply contextual interview each time, but the one skill I knew I had was to quickly get to the heart of what would be most important and most interesting for my audience, whether it was for the Today show, the midday radio news bulletin, or the top story on the 6pm TV news.

A lot of reporters at mainstream media titles will be part of a pool of general reporters. They'll report on a different topic area each day and won't necessarily have the detailed and contextual knowledge that specialist or niche reporters have. That said, just because an interviewer doesn't have a particular round, doesn't mean an interview with them will be easy. Experienced interviewers like Leigh Sales or Tracy Grimshaw for example, don't specialise in one field, but their interviewing technique is always forensic and thorough. You will find the same with some talk radio interviewers or podcast hosts.

Not here to make friends

When you interact with a reporter, neither of you are entering the relationship with the intention of making a new friend. Both of you have a business imperative at the heart of the interaction, and you're using each other to achieve your respective goals. On the reporter's side, they want to use you to help them tell a story that their audience will like and their boss will love. On your side, you want to use their publication to share your important messages with their large audience.

An interaction with a reporter should be like any other positive and courteous business interaction, and should be approached with the knowledge that an interview can have mutual benefits for both of you. As with any person you encounter in any other aspect of your working life, there'll be some reporters you genuinely warm to and others you just don't like, and that's perfectly OK. If you don't like them, you can still have a courteous and professional interview, keeping in mind that you're only interacting for the purpose of reaching that reporter's audience.

But who knows, you might make a friend out of it anyway!

You're not friends, but it is a relationship

I can't underestimate how important it is to grow relationships with reporters, producers, and other newsroom staff. Relationships with journalists should be fostered and nurtured, like any other professional relationship. You never know when your connection will come in handy.

At times your relationship with reporters may be adversarial, but it is still important to have a basic level of trust and mutual respect. Your willingness to front up and be interviewed about a difficult topic may make it easier for you to have a more proactive story published in the future. If you give great, quotable interviews with reporters, they are much more likely to want to interview you again down the track.

If you haven't worked with a particular reporter before, you'd be well advised to look into the type of stories they've worked on in the past, especially if they have a specialist round. This will give you a sense of their areas of interest, potential lines of questioning, and how they might frame a story. I'd encourage you to start becoming familiar with the work of all the specialist reporters in your industry. Perhaps follow them on social media and you will get a good sense of the articles that they work on and share. One of the reasons that a strong communications team or consultant is valuable is because of their existing relationships with a range of reporters, which you can benefit from.

After a story has been published or broadcast, there's no harm in dropping the reporter a quick note saying you read or saw it and wishing them all the best. If you didn't like the story, don't give them a piece of your mind. Move on with your life and focus on making the next story better.

What do they want the most?

What reporters are looking for, above all else, is a story. They love a good yarn! But what you think is a story, and what they think is a story, are probably quite different. They want a story that is exclusive to them, that will interest their readers or viewers, and will earn them praise from their boss. Remember a reporter isn't your paid public relations representative and isn't there to do your marketing for you. What is a big deal to you or your company, may not be a big deal to them or their audience. The challenge for you and your communications consultant or team is to discover and generate stories within your organisation that will be a hit with journalists. Part of doing so is considering whether the audience for a program or publication will really care about your story. Will it interest, engage and excite them? Will they tell other people about it? Be brutally honest about this before pitching a story. Because rest assured, a reporter will be brutally honest in saying no to your pitch if it isn't the right fit.

They want someone to talk to

One of the biggest mistakes an organisation can make when pitching a story to a journalist is not having a competent spokesperson available and willing to be interviewed at short notice. TV reporters need spokespeople (sometimes known as talking heads) to be interviewed to form part of the story. Radio producers are looking for interview talent for their talkback hosts to talk to. Print and online reporters will want unique quotes for their article. A media release with no spokesperson available? That's not a good idea.

Meet their deadlines and be accessible

If a spokesperson is going to agree to be interviewed, it's best to let the reporter know this as early as possible. If you leave it too late, you might be left out of the story altogether. If they've given you a deadline, don't wait right until the deadline to talk to them. Speak to them well in advance of it, if possible. If you decide that you're not going to participate in the story, let the reporter know that early, too. It's polite and courteous and will strengthen your relationship for the future. It's also worth remembering that in an era of rolling bulletins, social media and online news, reporters' deadlines are much shorter and more immediate than ever before. You may not have much time to make a decision.

You aren't much help to a reporter if you are not willing to be interviewed by them or if you ignore them altogether, and they won't be much help to you. Answering and returning their phone calls is important, and avoiding the media isn't a way to avoid a story being written about you. In fact, it's a sure way to guarantee a story is written about you without your input. Yes, there may be times that a decision is made to decline an interview request, but in most cases it's worthwhile to engage with the reporter on at least some level.

Making their life easier will make your life easier

The easier you can make a reporter's job, the more likely they will tell your story and tell it well. Helping a reporter is about more than just giving an interview. Together with your communications team, you should be offering to supplement your interview with high quality visual opportunities, photos, video or infographics. You might even suggest a case study who will be willing to be interviewed too.

Reporters don't want to interview boring, meandering spokespeople who never get to the point. They want interview subjects who are sharp, concise and laser-focused on the topic, who are interesting and engaging. Remember, just doing an interview is no guarantee that your comments will be included in the finished story. You absolutely must be memorable. And if you're memorable, the reporter will return to you for more stories in the future. A whole chapter later in this book is dedicated to how you can become a memorable interview subject.

Show caution and discretion

It's important to exercise a degree of caution when talking to reporters, too. You ought to consider that everything you say to a reporter is "on the record" and could be quoted. This includes general chit-chat before and after the interview, over the phone or via email. It's not uncommon for interview subjects to read a quote from themselves in print and say: "I didn't think that was part of the interview, we were just chatting!" The truth is, unless specified, there's no official start and end to an interview. Anything you say can be reported on. You should be cordial, polite, warm and friendly, but you must also take an "always on" approach to not disclosing trade secrets or letting your guard down around a reporter. This is true anywhere. Even at events, conferences, if you bump into them at a bar or if you're seated next to them at a dinner party. Be very careful.

Prepare in advance

Your best shot at having a great interaction with a reporter will only come when you've adequately prepared for an interview. In the next section of the book, I share a 5-step framework for getting ready for any interview. The 5 "prep steps" are simple enough that anyone should be able to remember them:

1. Ask some questions
2. Set a goal
3. Choose key messages
4. Make it memorable
5. Practice

Now let me walk you through them, one by one.

4.

PREP STEP ONE: ASK SOME QUESTIONS

Stop!

Yeah, that's right. Big red light. STOP!

Before diving headlong into a media interview, it's important that you STOP and ask some questions of your own, long before a journalist starts to ask them of you. If you're approached for an interview by a reporter, there are three key questions you need to ask yourself before doing anything else.

Question 1: Am I authorised to comment?

You certainly shouldn't be giving any interviews or speaking on behalf of your organisation unless you have authority to do so. Some members of the team, like the CEO, might have standing authorisation to speak, while others do not. Most members of your staff won't have permission to give interviews. And even if you are authorised to give an interview, before you do, you need to get to the next question...

Question 2: Have I alerted my communications team?

Often your communications team or consultant will take the first call or enquiry from the journalist anyway. Their contact details should be on your website and they are the people who journalists should be calling first. But occasionally, journalists will try to cut out the middle-man or middle-woman and will contact you directly by phone or email (mobile numbers are easy to find these days, and many executives are searchable on platforms such as LinkedIn). You should always alert your communications team as soon as you are aware of a media request before going ahead and doing the interview.

Question 3: Is there a broader context that I don't know about?

One danger of jumping straight into interviews is the risk that there may be some additional context surrounding the story that you don't know, or some other issues circulating that you need to become familiar with first. Taking a moment to check with your communications team will ensure that you're not caught commenting on the fly, without the full details in front of you.

PRO TIP: Buy yourself some time

Journalists are very good at trying to get a comment out of you on the spot, or right away over the phone. They'll assure you that their question is quick and it will help if you answer straight away. They'll even play the sympathy card, telling you their boss is breathing down their neck for a response. Reacting quickly to requests from journalists is important, but so is giving yourself time to prepare for questions.

If you're contacted directly, it can be a good idea to let the reporter know that you are very keen to talk, but aren't able to at this very second. Let them know you understand the urgency and will return their call shortly. If you need an excuse, you can tell them you're with someone at this very moment (and in fact, you may well be!). Make sure you grab their details, and immediately contact your communications team or consultant. Doing so will buy you some time to consider your response and your team can look after the administrative side of things, including setting up an interview time and helping you prepare.

If you've decided it's a good idea to go ahead with the interview (and we discussed earlier in the book some of the times you might decline), the next set of questions deals with the nuts and bolts of interview logistics. If you have a communications team or consultant, they can help answer these questions. To help you adequately prepare, you need to be asking:

- Who?
- What?
- When?
- Where?
- Why?

Who is it with and who is it for?

When it comes to "who", there are actually two questions.

First, who is it with? Earlier we discussed that knowing whether your interviewer is a specialist or a general reporter will help you prepare. It will also give you a sense of the forum, such as whether it's a TV interview or print interview, and whether it will be live or pre-recorded. Knowing who the interview is with, and being familiar with that interviewer's style is an important part of your preparation. It can also give you an idea of the type of questions they might ask. You should also have an understanding of their publication or the show that they work on. You'll prepare very differently for a chat with a morning TV show, for example, than you will for an in-depth discussion with a reporter from a high-profile finance publication.

Second, who is it for? It's easy to get carried away with who the journalist is, and overlook *who really matters* in the interview. It's not the reporter. It's not you either.

The audience matters the most. That is who you're really talking to. Regardless of whether the interview is with an investigator from Four Corners, the brekkie bunch from an FM radio station or an influencer with their own podcast, you must never forget that the point of your communication is getting a message across to an audience. Although you might be looking at the reporter when you give your answers, you're really talking to their audience.

It's crucial to think carefully about precisely who makes up the audience before the interview. What's important to them? What will they be interested in? What would they want to know from you? How can you help them?

Visualise your audience. Where are they and what are they doing when they are reading your comments or watching your interview? Are they:

- A mum or dad listening to the radio on the school run?
- A retiree reading a broadsheet newspaper over breakfast in the morning?
- A student reading the article on their phone on the way to uni?
- A tech geek reading a niche website?
- An office worker checking the headlines on their computer at lunchtime?
- A podcast devotee who listens to this program every week?
- An office worker watching a breakfast TV show

before their commute?

- A politics enthusiast watching a panel debate show?
- An investor who subscribes to a specialist share market publication?

Depending on the program or publication the audience might be very broad or very niche, and you should take that into account when preparing. Remember, interviewers usually know the demographics and interests of their audiences well and are often advocates for them, so they will be asking you questions that are relevant to that particular audience. The interview is for the audience. It should be focused on *their* needs, wants, curiosities and interests.

> **PRO TIP: An interview is not a contest**
>
> Competitive interviewees often treat interviews as a contest to be won or lost. They get their back up when they don't like an interviewer's questions and can become aggressive or try to show them up. They forget what message they're trying to get across and attempt to win at all costs. It's usually a terrible tactic that makes them look bad.
>
> "I showed them!" they think, at the end. But all they really showed was that they had forgotten about the audience, and focused only on the interviewer. Most

likely, the audience formed a very different view of the interviewee.

I'm not saying that you need to be a pushover if you're attacked or if a reporter presents information or opinions that aren't accurate, but just remember if you're too aggressive the audience will judge you for it.

What is it about?

Is this a proactive story or reactive story? Is the story already out there in the media or will this be the first time people learn about it?

If the story is a proactive one where you've sought publicity, you'll know in advance what it's about. In fact, you may have been involved in the pitch, perhaps helped craft the media release, and will be across most of the details.

If it's a reactive story, your preparation may be trickier. If you have a communications team or consultant, they can help you prepare by gathering information that gets to the core of what the story is really about. The team might even garner some of this information through a prior discussion or background briefing with the reporter. You can't ask reporters for a full list of the questions they're planning to ask — that's a big no-no in most reporters' books — but it's certainly OK to get a general sense of the topics they want to cover.

Where is it going to take place?

This might seem like a boring part of logistics, but the interview location will certainly impact your preparation. Will you need to travel into a TV studio or will a reporter and camera operator come to you? Knowing where the interview will take place will affect how you dress and prepare on the day, and also impact your diary and calendar schedule. If it's a radio interview, will it be over the phone or at the station? If it's via phone, do you have a quiet area of your home or office where you can talk uninterrupted? If you're going to have visitors to your work premises, have you alerted security and reception? Has your communications team or consultant scoped a suitable and quiet location? A reason to be on top of boring logistics is so that uncertainty or worry around these small details doesn't contribute to any additional nerves closer to your interview. If all the small details are covered, you can then focus on the big ones!

When is it going to be conducted?

Earlier in the book, I mentioned the importance of building relationships with reporters. Knowing when the interview is scheduled and showing the courtesy of being ready at the appointed time is an important part of maintaining a strong relationship with them into the future. If you've cancelled, been late, or rescheduled an interview, a reporter may have second thoughts about wanting to talk to you next time. Sometimes reporters will be a little inflexible about when they can interview you. This might be due to resources such as the availability of camera crews and photographers, the constraints of the program they work on, or the deadlines they are working to. If an interview is important to you, you may need to be flexible. If you're not, they'll find another interviewee who isn't such a headache to work with.

When it comes to broadcast interviews, you may need to be available well in advance of the actual interview time slot. If your slot on a TV panel show is at 7pm, for example, you may need to arrive at the studios at 6pm so that you can visit the make-up department. If your radio slot is at 3.15pm, the producer of the program may want you on the phone and ready to go at 3.05pm, just so there are no technical problems.

If you know an interview is scheduled for a certain time, you should also clear plenty of time in your diary before it to allow for last-minute preparation and rehearsals. This will help you to feel calm and in control. You don't want to be sweatily racing out of an important meeting with colleagues on another topic, and straight into an interview without a chance to compose yourself, rehearse and check your appearance. You want to be fresh and focussed when you take part in any interview.

Why am I doing this anyway?

This is the most important question of all. In fact, it's so important, that the next chapter is devoted entirely to it.

Why?

5.

PREP STEP TWO: SET A GOAL

Why are you doing this?

You don't give media interviews as a favour to reporters. And you don't give them just because they asked politely. You give media interviews because, selfishly, there's something in it for your organisation, a net-benefit if you like.

What is your reason for doing the interview? It should be because you want the audience to feel a certain way, know a certain thing, or take a certain action as a result of what you've said in the interview. This is the goal.

I like to think of the goal as "the bigger picture", and everything else as "the finer details". Both are important. But we can't have details without understanding the bigger picture first.

The goal of an interview should be simple and straightforward. Sometimes, it might be as simple as:

- "We want to sell more tickets to the game."
- "We want people to know we have a new range of shoes."
- "We want help to solve a crime."
- "We want people to buy our album."
- "We want people to know we've stuffed up, but we're taking responsibility for it."
- "We want people to believe we're spending their taxes wisely."

Notice there's no real supporting detail in the goals above, and that's OK. All of the above are pretty broad statements and they're supposed to be. Don't worry, we'll get to adding finer details to support the goal in due course. (If you're impatient, those "finer details" are called key messages and we get to them in the very next chapter!).

An exhausting example

The best way I can help you understand how to frame a goal is with an example. Let us for a moment imagine a car company has discovered that its latest model has rolled off the production line with a problem in its exhaust system. The company has had to issue a recall notice, and all the affected vehicles need to be brought in by their customers for repairs. It's not a safety issue, as such, but it will definitely cause inconvenience to customers. The brand's reputation is at stake, and its customers' loyalty will be strained. The media is circling, and refusing interviews could make the company appear evasive and damage its reputation even further.

So what should the company's goal be here? What's the bigger picture for them? You'd think a goal at the top of the list might be "we want to reassure customers that they can trust us". (The bottom line, of course, is if the company can't be trusted, people will stop buying their cars!)

Notice the goal doesn't refer to the details of the recall specifically, or the practicalities of what customers need to do to get their car fixed. Of course these finer details are important and they'll definitely form the substance of what the spokesperson will actually say in the interview. The goal is always at a larger, sometimes even more philosophical level. It's asking yourself how you want the audience to think, feel and act as a result of what you say in the interview. It's the bigger picture. Never forget it.

The essence of the interview

You'll notice the goal I gave for the motor company above contained some important keywords or buzzwords . In the example, they were words such as "reassurance", "confidence" and "trust". If you're ever having difficulty nailing what the goal for your interview should be, try to think of the values you'd like the audience to associate with you, or with the issue you are discussing. In a crisis, those values might be trustworthiness, safety, seriousness or credibility. For the launch of a new product the values might be excitement, fascination or joy. If you've made a mistake, the values might be apology and acknowledgment. These keywords should form part of your nominated goal and are really the essence of the interview.

People reading, watching or listening to you probably won't remember every single point that you make in an interview. They may not remember every tiny detail you added, every statistic or every anecdote. But they will remember, in a broader sense, how you made them feel, and hopefully the action you want them to take. By thinking in these bigger picture terms, we're actually cutting to the core of why we're giving an interview in the first place.

Keep the goal simple

With no goal, you have no direction. But by having a goal, you have a purpose and can more easily prepare for an interview. The specifics of what you will say, the tone with which you say it, the examples or case studies you use and everything else all flow from the central goal. Keep your goal simple. Once you know what it is, you can move on to the finer details. We call these the key messages, and the next chapter is focussed on them.

6.

PREP STEP THREE: CHOOSE KEY MESSAGES

We know where we're going but how do we get there?

Once we have a goal, we have a destination in mind. But what about the finer details of how to actually get there? A map would be handy! The map in this case, is made up of our key messages. Key messages are sometimes called talking points. In the most simple terms, these are the most important concepts, key points or ideas that you really want the audience to know about the topic.

What you want the audience to know will vary from interview to interview, depending upon the style, the publication, the audience and other factors. Preparing messages means you come to an interview ready with things to say, regardless of the questions the reporter might ask.

If you have a communications team or consultant, they will help you formulate your key messages for any interview.

And there's more help from me below. But in the meantime, let me help you understand key messages a little better by revisiting the example of the car company and its exhaust dilemma.

Some exhausting messages

OK, so the car company is continuing to deal with a crisis situation. It's had to issue a recall of an important model, and is dealing with the customer fallout. But the company wants to be open and honest with its customers and share critical information with them. The company has agreed to a number of interviews, including a TV interview with a major broadcaster. We know its goal is to foster trust among customers. But what are the key messages to share with customers so that they can feel this trust?

In this case, those messages might be:

- We apologise to our loyal customers and we've moved fast to solve this problem.
- Having your vehicle repaired is a simple process, which will take less than 30 minutes at your nearest dealer.
- We acknowledge the inconvenience and will provide a loan car for any customer who needs one while their car is being repaired.
- We always put our customers first, which is why so many Australians have put their trust in us for over 50 years.

This is a good list, but not necessarily an exhaustive one. (Sorry for the pun...or am I?!) If you worked for the car company in this example, would you use different messages?

They're for positive stories too

Key messages aren't just for negative, reactive stories. They're for positive and proactive stories too. Let's fast-forward in time, and imagine that our car manufacturer's problems have been solved, the cars have been repaired, consumers have forgiven them and the company is now planning a proactive series of stories and interviews for an exciting new model just about to be released. The goal for the interviews is to get the audience excited about the new vehicle and encourage them to visit a dealer for a test drive.

All sorts of media across the spectrum have requested interviews. So the key messages will need to be tailored for each individual interview.

For a specialist, niche, car publication, the key messages might be:

- The engine has 800 Nm of torque.
- It can go 0-100km in five seconds.
- A fuel hybrid model will also be available.

But for an interview with a finance reporter who has a different audience, the key messages might be different:

- Our entry-level model is the most affordable in its

class.

- The company is expecting sales of the car to boost its fourth quarter profits.
- It's manufactured in Korea, reducing some production costs.

Notice the messaging is tailored uniquely for each interview. A one-size-fits-all approach will never achieve the best results.

Enough about cars, what about your key messages?

How do you decide on key messages for your own brand, organisation or situation? A good technique I learnt a long time ago is to pause for a moment and ask yourself a simple question:

> *"If I'm quoted on just a couple of things from this interview, what do I want them to be?"*

It's a way to get to the heart of what's important and decide on your key messages. The truth is, in some interviews you *will* only be quoted on a couple of things you've said. In fact, perhaps just one! To be well prepared, you'll want to come armed with a small collection of messages, all of which will support you in achieving your goal for the interview, whatever that goal might be.

I would aim for three key messages if you're just getting started, and definitely no more than six, even if you're very experienced at interviews. Having too many messages to remember is too difficult, and risks diluting the most important ones.

Key messages should be simple, easy to remember and straightforward. They should:

- Be only one sentence each (around 10 seconds long).
- Be in plain English, free of jargon and technical language.
- Be very clear and easy to remember.
- Sound interesting when said aloud.
- Be tailored to the sort of questions that are likely to be asked.

But above all, they must be:

- Something you want the audience to know.

And:

- Something that the audience will care about.

When you brainstorm your key messages, you might find yourself with a list of 10 possible messages, or perhaps more. You will need to cull. You must refine and reduce them. Use the above checklist to help determine if they should be included at all. Pay particular attention to the very last couple of points above. Are your messages something that your audience either needs to know or will really, genuinely care about? Remember this interview is about what they want to hear, not just about what you want to say.

If you're still having trouble reducing your messages, brutally prioritise them from most to least important. Having too many messages will only serve to confuse you.

But I have so much to say! Why should I dumb it down so much?

Media stories are not technical papers or academic journals. They are not entire books or encyclopaedias of knowledge on a topic area. When you condense your knowledge of a topic to the most important parts for a media interview, you are doing your audience a favour and respecting the limitations of the forum in which you are communicating. This isn't about dumbing down. It's about using language the audience will understand in the forum that you've found yourself in.

Interviews are often very short anyway. You are much better to make a small number of points and make them well, than deliver a laundry list of information that overwhelms the audience. In an interview setting, less really is more. Also, having fewer messages means that you will have more opportunity to repeat them. The repetition of key messages means they are much more likely to become embedded in the memory of the audience.

And at the end of the day, the more you try to remember, the more likely you are to become stressed, anxious or nervous leading up to the interview, just like studying for an exam back in your school days. You should be trying to make the job of participating in an interview easier for yourself, not harder. And don't forget, audience members who are intrigued by the interview can always seek out additional information by contacting your business, visiting your website and so forth.

Delivering your messages

Your key messages won't be the only things you talk about in an interview. Sometimes the interview will stray onto other topics and you might talk about other things depending on where the questions lead you. That's OK. What's most important though, is that you work on incorporating your key messages into your answers at various stages of the interview.

Your primary key message should be repeated at least once during your interview and ideally several times. This repetition makes it clear to the interviewer and to the audience that it is an important point, especially when they hear it said more than once. Moreover though, the repetition means the message is more likely to stick in their mind once the interview is complete. We don't want to overdo it with repetition either though, as admittedly, anything repeated far too much can sound boring. This is why we come to an interview armed with a selection of key messages to sprinkle through our delivery. Variety is the spice of life!

Your crash mat

I like to the think of key messages as being the ultimate

crash mat. An interview can be a dangerous, high-wire act, but if you've prepared these safe topic areas to talk about, you will always have something to say, regardless of the nature of questions you are thrown, or if you lose your train of thought. You'll always have a crash mat to land on! I've also heard the analogy that key messages can be like a lifeboat. When you become lost, tongue-tied or go off track, returning to a key message is like getting into a lifeboat. You're safe, dry, and ready to have another go!

Forget word-perfect

You don't need to remember and deliver your key messages absolutely verbatim, word-for-word, each time. The most important thing is that you hit the core component, concepts or keywords from each message, and do it over and again. In fact, if you're able to vary the way you deliver the messages throughout the interview, but still get the essence of them across, you'll remain interesting to the audience while staying focused on your goal. And remember, your key messages are merely starting points for discussion. You can wrap more detail around and present them in slightly different ways in each interview. We keep them short and sweet so that they are easy to remember. In each interview, you will want to expand on them.

But key messages on their own can feel a little dry, prepared and rehearsed. How do we make them more memorable? The next chapter has all the answers.

7.

PREP STEP FOUR: MAKE IT MEMORABLE

You have to stand out

It's one thing to give an interview, but it's another thing altogether to give an interview that stands out and is remembered. One of the biggest challenges in a congested media world can be making sure that when you talk, people listen. Doing an interview with a reporter is no guarantee that your quotes will actually make it into the story. If you're boring, if you have no energy or if you don't say anything memorable, then your comments might not make it into the final edit. What a waste of time that would be! Our next challenge is to make key messages really shine, by turning them into something truly memorable.

There are many ways that we can transform our key messages to make them really stand out and be memorable. I like to break these techniques into:

- News grabs
- Storytelling
- Statistics
- Speech

News grabs

News grabs (also called "sound bites" in broadcasting or "key quotes" for print/online stories), are pre-prepared, pithy statements that use clever language to capture the essence of a key message in a short, memorable collection of words that sounds pleasant to the ear. Reporters are always listening with a finely tuned ear to pick out and use the more interesting news grabs from all the commentary that is shared in an interview. Put simply, news grabs, sound bites or key quotes make your key messages stand out.

If you can come up with a memorable news grab to partner with a key message, you are well on your way to ensuring it will form part of the story. There are no guarantees of course, but the more memorable it is, the more likely the reporter will include it. Good politicians are particularly adept at understanding the value of a memorable news grab. They know that a TV reporter, for example, can't include their whole press conference in a story on the 6pm news. The reporter will only be able to use the most memorable 10-second news grab in their report. So, in advance, the politician, together with their advisors, will work on crafting some news grabs to be weaved into the politicians' answers. And voila! They appear on the news at night, summing up their whole message in one pithy line/sound bite/news grab/quote.

These clever lines usually don't come to a spokesperson on the spot. They're the result of careful planning. But there are lots of ways to create effective news grabs that you can use for yourself.

Absolute language

Speaking with authority through no-nonsense language brings additional gravitas to what you're saying and makes people stop and listen. Using words like "always", "must", "never, ever", or "have to" brings a sense of certainty, strength and power to your words.

So instead of:

> *"Investing is a path to fiscal autonomy, and although there are caveats, the present market demonstrates key opportunities which hitherto haven't existed."*

You could try:

> *"There has **never been a better time** to start investing."*

Emotion

Depending on the topic you are being interviewed about, using some emotion in your delivery can help humanise the issue and build a connection. It can show that you're on the side of the audience and understand how they're feeling. You can use language carefully to convey emotions such as frustration, anger, disappointment, fury or joy.

So instead of:

> "The 8% tax increase will create division and discord in the community due to the overwhelming pressures engulfing wage-workers who are struggling against market forces."

You could try:

> "The decision is a **kick in the guts** for hard working Aussies who are just trying to make a living."

Cliches

Our English teachers in high school told us to avoid clichés (like the plague!), but they can actually be a very succinct way to make a key point. The benefit of clichés is that a few words can encapsulate a much greater meaning.

So instead of:

> "Detectives will canvass all possibilities and will consider all avenues, including substantive profiles of key witnesses and persons of interest."

You could try:

> "We're going to leave **no stone unturned** in this investigation."

Alliteration

Alliteration is when a group of words in succession all have the same first letter. The repeated sounds give greater emphasis and the rhythm captures the attention of the viewer, listener or reader.

So instead of:

> "There is a demand in secondary education for improvement in key growth areas. Among these are a greater quantity of experienced educators, ongoing developmental growth for leaders and a scope of digital products that will enhance the learning experience."

You could try:

> "Our high school principals need three things: more **t**eachers, more **t**raining and more **t**echnology."

Analogy

An analogy is when you use a comparison between your issue and a similar situation that people are more familiar with and can relate to better. It's important not to overuse analogies but sometimes they can work well to make a sharp point.

So instead of:

> "The Treasurer has demonstrated a high degree of incompetence in failing to drive the impetus to improve the substandard state of our economy."

You could try:

> "If your **car's broken, you get it fixed**. Well our economy is broken and the Treasurer is doing nothing to fix it."

Numbers

The last thing you want to do is bombard your audience with numbers and statistics that will confuse them, but when used effectively, they can help support the points you are trying to make. The key is making sure that any numbers you include make it easier to understand your key messages, not more confusing.

So instead of:

> "The annual impost of the new bargaining agreement for cleaning personnel will be in the degree of 8%, which is why we will lodge legal proceedings in the appropriate time frame in order to seek a more satisfactory resolution."

You could try:

> "I'm furious our hardworking cleaners will be **$200** worse off each month. That's **200 reasons** why we're appealing this decision."

Repetition

If there's one keyword that underpins or embodies your entire message, then simply repeating it can make it resonate with people who are listening. Make sure you pepper that word through everything you're saying. This is especially true for strong, conceptual words like trust, safety, privacy and so forth.

So instead of:

> *"It was thought that we would be incapable of achieving an outcome, and there was significant doubt from stakeholders that we were capable of providing their desired outcome in the long term."*

You could try:

> *"They've **trusted** our decision. They've **trusted** us to deliver. And they've **trusted** that we'll see it through."*

Rhythm and rhyme

The reason we remember nursery rhymes from childhood, the lyrics of a song, or the words of a favourite poem are in large part due to their rhythm and rhyme. You have to be careful. Used poorly, this technique will make you sound like you're reciting an advertising jingle. But used sparingly and carefully, rhythm and rhyme can really help you hit your mark.

So instead of:

> *"Prolonged exposure to ultraviolet rays inevitably leads to increased risk of cancer exposure."*

You could try:

> *"There's nothing **fun** about spending too long in the **sun**."*

Just the beginning

Of course, you shouldn't just talk in news grabs alone. You'll almost always need to give more detail in all your answers so that the reporter has some context and understands the issue fully. But a news grab can be a great way to start off or wrap up a sentence.

To understand how it might work in practice, let's imagine a personal trainer is being interviewed about weight loss. Here's part of their interview:

> Reporter:
> *"What is the most effective way to lose weight?"*
>
> Personal trainer:
> *"It's all about energy in and energy out, that's where you get the clout. What I mean by that is that all food we eat contains calories, which are really just energy. The more food we eat, the more calories we take in. But when we exercise, we use up some of that energy. The more exercise we do, the more calories we burn. We want to burn more calories than we eat to lose weight. That's why I like to say energy in and energy out, that's where you get the clout."*

Note that the trainer provided a really good news grab, and repeated it at the start and end of the answer, but also gave some extra information and context.

You should come armed with two or three news grabs for each interview so that you can offer some variety. Once you get more experienced at knowing the types of news grabs that reporters like to hear, creating them will become far easier for you. To become better at this, start watching the nightly news more closely and observe the news grabs that reporters select from interviewees. By paying closer attention you'll get to know what makes a good news grab.

Storytelling

Another way you can bring a key message to life in an interview is by telling a brief anecdote or story that references your key messages or is consistent with the same values.

When you tell a story, you humanise the topic and transport the listener or viewer to another place and time. This helps them to absorb the message by visualising it and connecting with it. The story might be about you, or perhaps it might be about a customer, a client, or someone you've encountered in your work. You might even retell a story that has been shared with you by someone else, acknowledging its source, of course.

Imagine, for example, an interview with the director of a program for at-risk youth, who wants to convey the message that their intervention program is effective at turning around the lives of young people. Just saying this isn't quite enough. Where's the proof?

The message of success can be conveyed with so much more passion and vigour, and will be more likely to be remembered by your audience if you tell a brief story that encapsulates it instead.

Compare this statement:

> "We get great results with young people, because we go to great lengths to help them."

With sharing this story:

> *"One of the young people who joined our young program really stands out. Matt had come from a broken home and grew up around drugs and domestic abuse. He was mixing with the wrong crowd, and had already been in court for some petty crimes. When I first met him he didn't want to know anything about me. But day by day, I was able to connect with him. Within a couple of months he was back in school, and last year he got his HSC. The phone rang the other day and it was Matt. 'I just want to thank you for believing in me.' He's doing an apprenticeship to become a plumber, and has goals of running his own business. Matt is living proof that our program works. I'm so proud of him."*

Telling the story took the listener on a journey, put a human face on the program and helped build an emotional connection.

Storytelling works well when you can bring the story to life in just a few sentences. You don't want to tell stories that go on and on; you really do need to get to the point quickly. Longer form live interviews are the best format for storytelling. What's most important is that your story supports your key messages and that you've ensured that you're in the correct interview situation to tell it well.

Your organisation may well have evergreen stories and case studies that you can incorporate into a range of different interviews at different times. You need to plan storytelling in advance. It's rare to come up with the right story on the spot!

Statistics

We're always looking for proof if someone makes a bold claim, and experienced interviewers will always seek to call out interview subjects who can't back up what they're saying with clear evidence. This is one area where statistics as proof-points can really help.

So, in an interview where you are talking about your company's new app, rather than saying:

> *"Lots of people have been downloading our app."*

You would be much better off saying:

> *"We had more than 100,000 downloads on the first day, which is a record for a new developer."*

Note in this example, that not only is the actual figure (100,000 downloads) included, but also some additional context ("a record for a new developer"), which explains why the number is important. Just throwing figures out there, unless they mean something to the audience, renders them boring and pointless. People unfamiliar with the industry might not know if 100,000 downloads is impressive, so you need to tell them.

With statistics, it's important that you don't just bamboozle people with numbers. If you do, your audience will become overwhelmed. If using statistics, you need to use them in a way that the audience understands, and on a level that affects them.

So, if a government minister is announcing a new welfare package, instead of saying:

> "The package is worth $700 million for families across Australia."

They would make more impact if they said:

> "We're helping one million Aussie families, and they'll each be $700 better off."

And if a beer company is boasting about its sales, instead of just saying:

> "We sold 42,000 kegs of beer."

They might say:

> "We sold 42,000 kegs. That's enough beer to fill an Olympic swimming pool!"

Speech

Finally, when it comes to delivering a key message, it's not just what you say, but how you say it that matters too. How fast you talk, where you put your emphasis, where you choose to pause, how loud you talk, and your tone will all have an impact on the effectiveness of your interview. In fact speech, and other presentation skills are so important that they get their own chapter later in the book, so stay tuned. But we've got just a couple more steps to cover before then.

8.

PREP STEP FIVE: PRACTICE

Be honest

When people tell me they've been disappointed with their performance in a media interview, I often ask how many times they practiced delivering their key messages to a colleague or friend.

"Did you rehearse?" I ask.

"No," they often say sheepishly. Some add, "I know in training you said I should, but I didn't have the time!"

If you don't have time to practice, you don't have time to give an interview! Rehearsal is the final hurdle of interview preparation, and the stage of preparation that's most likely to lead to the biggest improvement, yet it is the stage that so many people choose to skip. Skipping rehearsals is done at your own peril. Going headlong into an interview without any practice is foolhardy and dangerous.

Say it out loud

Here's the situation. You're a busy executive with an interview coming up, but fortunately you have the support of your communications team or consultant to work on some great key messages for your interview. You trust their judgment and wait for their email with the talking points and suggested sound bites to come through. You're very busy, but you have a quick read of the document in the taxi while on your way to the interview.

What could possibly go wrong? Well, everything really. Because glancing down at your smartphone for five minutes isn't a rehearsal.

Seeing words on paper, or on a smartphone screen, and reading them to yourself in your head does little to help you commit them to memory. You'll never know if the words are the right fit for you unless you say them aloud. Rehearsing out loud gives you an opportunity to see if the messages roll off your tongue and sound natural and conversational. I bet if someone has written them for you, when you say them out loud you might even change a word or two if it's not quite the right fit for you. Personalising the messages so that they're a natural fit for your delivery style is particularly important.

Now add some questions

But saying the messages out loud isn't enough. An actual interviewer isn't going to say to you: "Thanks for your time, could you just read out your corporate messages for me one-by-one from your prepared notes please? I'd like to test your memory."

An interview requires you to answer questions, which means thinking on your feet and adapting quickly. Before any interview, you absolutely must have a colleague, friend, or ideally a member of your communications team or your consultant grill you as if it were a real interview. And what's most important? You need to record it and watch it back.

You don't need a full camera crew like the ones we have in our in-person media training sessions. Just using a smartphone is fine. By watching back your performance, you will be able to see for yourself how you are delivering your answers and whether you are really nailing those key messages. You will soon discover if you have made them too wordy or too difficult to get across. You'll notice moments where you need to improve, but also see the areas where you shine. This should give you the encouragement you need to know you can handle the interview.

Then turn up the heat

Encourage your mock interviewer to increase the difficulty of their questions as you spend more time practicing. Their perspective may help you prepare for some questions that you hadn't anticipated and may lead to workshopping or refining some of your responses. There's an entire chapter later in this book dedicated to how to handle difficult questions, which will help you with a framework for answering these.

When anticipating what the difficult questions might be,

you need to think like a journalist for a minute. What do you think they would want to know? What questions would their audience expect them to ask? How could they try to trip you up? Remember, it's not their job to go easy on you. Their job is to get answers and get a good story. Put yourself in their shoes and consider how they might try to achieve that.

Practicing for and anticipating all these possibilities in advance should give you the confidence to know you've done all you can to prepare for the interview.

If you haven't prepared, practiced and rehearsed? Well, you've only got yourself to blame if something goes wrong. Sorry, I meant *when* something goes wrong.

9.

THE PREP STEPS IN ACTION: A CASE STUDY

The scenario

A major celebrity has released a statement announcing complications from being diagnosed with skin cancer. The celebrity says that they are going to be OK, but is urging everyone, everywhere, to have their skin checked. Because the celebrity is so well known, their plight has become a talking point, and as a result, their story and the issue of melanoma is being widely discussed in the media.

The general manager of a large charity that raises money for research into skin cancer has been invited on an afternoon talk-radio program to discuss the issues that the star's diagnosis has raised and what the public ought to know. The manager and her team have only a short window of preparation time, but realise that it is important that the organisation is part of big conversations on the issue.

The 5 Steps

Step 1: Ask some questions

The GM and team workshop the invitation quickly and agree immediately that it is a good idea to do the radio interview, as it will draw valuable attention to the issue, get the charity's name out there in the public eye, and might also help with fundraising efforts. Through the quick team workshop, these key questions have been answered:

> **Who is it with?**
> The afternoon show host on Radio 2GB.
>
> **Who is it really for?**
> Listeners whose lives may be affected by skin cancer.
>
> **What is it?**
> A live-to-air talkback radio interview about skin cancer, in light of the recent celebrity diagnosis.
>
> **Where is it going to be held?**
> Via telephone to the radio studio from the GM's office.
>
> **When is it going to take place?**
> The interview is at 4.10pm. Producers in the studio will call the office line at 4.05pm.
>
> **Why are we doing it?**
> To raise awareness of the practical things people can do to prevent skin cancer.

Step 2: Set a goal

As part of team discussions, it was agreed that the goal of the interview should not be to focus on the celebrity angle of the story, but rather to move the issue on and inform people of the simple, practical steps they can take to protect themselves from skin cancer.

Step 3: Choose key messages

With the above goal in mind, the team and GM were able to agree upon three key messages:

1. Australians can help prevent skin cancer by wearing a hat, using sunscreen and staying out of the sun during the hottest part of the day.
2. Skin cancer can be treated, but only when diagnosed early, which is why visiting a doctor for regular skin checks is important.
3. Modern research is helping with new prevention and treatment methods, and donations to our charity will help this life saving work.

Step 4: Make it memorable

The team decided that it was important to have some strong sound bites that would support the key messages they wanted to get across. They decided that the GM would try to include some of the following sound bites in her answers:

> *"As we always say, there's nothing fun about spending too long in the sun."*

> "We see one thousand new skin cancer cases every day...that's a thousand reasons you should to go to your doctor and get a skin check."
>
> "Donations to skin cancer research save lives. It could be your mum's life, your brother's life or maybe even your own."

The team also decided that the GM might also tell a short story about her own experience with melanoma in her family, in order to personalise and humanise the story a little bit more.

Step 5: Practice

Preparation time was limited, but it was agreed that a couple of practice interviews in the office would help increase confidence going into the interview. The team recorded the audio using a smart phone and listened back to it together.

As part of the rehearsal, they also noted a couple of problem areas that the GM might face in terms of difficult questions including: "How much of the funds donated to the charity go to research and how much to staff salaries?"

Because the interview was to be a remote radio interview, and the GM would be allowed to have some notes available, the communications team prepared a cheat sheet with key messages and news grabs on it that she could refer to in an emergency if she got stuck during the interview.

How it went

The team was incredibly happy with how the interview went! At first, the interviewer was focusing heavily on the celebrity angle, but the GM was able to redirect the conversation back to the key messages around skin cancer awareness. She even got to include a couple of the prepared sound bites. She was glad she had rehearsed with the team, because the host of the show took some talkback callers who wanted to know whether the money from donations was really going to research purposes. The interview was a success, but only because of methodical preparation, and plenty of rehearsal.

10.

THE DIFFERENT INTERVIEWS YOU'LL FACE

Know the rules for the game you're going to play

Until this point in the book, we've discussed interviews quite broadly, without considering the many different types of interviews, and how your preparation and delivery needs to be adjusted to match each type. In a moment, we'll look at the different demands of TV, radio, print and online interviews. Each has different rules, parameters and possibilities. Regardless of the medium though, it's helpful to understand that interviews really boil down to two key types: live and pre-recorded

Live: Where they hear everything you say

By and large, the interviews where the audience hears absolutely everything you say are the ones that go live-to-air, usually for broadcast on television or radio, and these days, perhaps on live-streaming platforms or social media.

These interviews are a great chance to get more of your message across and give much greater depth and context. Because they are live, nothing can be edited out. There is less opportunity for you to claim that your words were twisted or taken out of context. This direct communication to your audience is the payoff you get for having to deal with the stress of a live interview, either conducted in a studio or as a live-cross to you at a remote location. They can vary in length, but most broadcast interviews are 3-5 minutes long.

Podcasts with longer recording times might be included in this category as well. Although they're not necessarily broadcast live, many podcast hosts will treat the recording "as live" and only perform minimal editing before distribution. It's worth checking whether a podcast will be edited or shortened before participating, so that you understand the process in advance.

Pre-recorded: Where they only hear, see or read snippets of what you say

If an interview isn't live, it will be pre-recorded. This means the journalist will select some, but not all, of your comments from the interview to include in the finished story.

Most interviews for online and print news articles, and television news and current affairs packages are conducted in this format. The reporter might ask you questions for 5-10 minutes, but when you see the final story, only a selection of your comments will be used, perhaps alongside the comments of other people who have also been interviewed for the story.

Interviewees are often disappointed when they are interviewed for such a long time, but only 10 seconds of what they say is used in the story. Having only a portion of your remarks included in the story can be frustrating, but it is the reality of news production. Commercial TV news stories only go for about 90 seconds and online news stories might only be a few hundred words. A reporter can't possibly use absolutely everything you say. Remember earlier in the book when we talked about the importance of sound bites? It's in this sort of interview that they are so crucial. Delivering strong sound bites which convey a lot of meaning in just a few words, will make it more likely that your key messages come across in the story.

Live TV interviews

Live television interviews take place either:

- In-person at the television studio with the host(s)
- At a remote studio in another location
- As a live-cross with a camera-operator sent to your home or office
- As a live-cross via an online app such as Skype or Zoom

Live TV in a studio with the interviewer

These sorts of interviews are common on breakfast television programs and also on 24-hour news channels. They usually last a few minutes and will involve a handful of questions. You might be seated at a desk or on a couch, so you should be aware of this when you are planning what to wear, as you may be visible from your shoes up. The segment may involve some interaction on the set, if required. For example, if you're a personal trainer, you might be asked to demonstrate some exercises. You will usually be aware of parameters like this well before the interview, so that you can prepare.

A producer will be assigned to your segment, and will be your main point of contact in the lead-up to your interview. The hosts are far too busy to manage the logistics of their program and usually have a large team working to put the show together. Your producer will let you know what time to arrive at the studio, and what time you will be on air. They will tell you whether hair and make-up will be provided, or if you need to arrive "camera ready". Make sure you ask the producer you've been dealing with any questions you may have, and keep their contact number handy in case you need to get in touch on the day of your appearance.

I recommend that you bring some additional make up for touch-ups (regardless of whether or not it will be provided) with you, as well as some tissues, a bottle of water, and any other items that you think you might need to make yourself comfortable. Make sure you give yourself plenty of time to get to the studio, accounting for traffic and parking difficulties. You don't want to miss your interview!

Every studio and set is different, but most will have a waiting area (sometimes called a green room), where you will pass the time before your segment. If other people are part of your segment (if it's a panel discussion for example), it's here you may have a chance to greet them and introduce yourself before being on-air together.

Before going onto the set, it's important to check your appearance in a mirror or even with the camera function of your smartphone. When you finish this check, make sure you switch your phone to silent. You don't want it ringing when you are on-air!

You will usually be brought onto the set during an ad break or while a pre-recorded segment is playing. Sometimes the hosts will be able to greet you and have a quick chat, but sometimes they will be pre-occupied, so don't be offended if they aren't too talkative with you before your segment. You may hear them talking to staff in the control room who speak to them via near-invisible earpieces.

Once in the studio, a technician may attach a lapel microphone to your clothing. If there isn't a suitable spot to clip the microphone to the outside of your clothing, they may ask politely if the microphone cable can be run up the inside of your clothing and attached with tape. Again, take this into consideration when deciding what you will wear, because microphones will sometimes have a battery pack that will need to clip to your outfit.

The set will usually have very bright lights, and although they may feel confronting at first, you will quickly get used to them and they are unlikely to affect your view of the hosts asking you questions. You will see a lot of cameras, and you will also notice some TV monitors with the program itself playing on them. You may even see a close-up of yourself on one of these monitors. Avoid the temptation to look at yourself on these monitors at any time during your appearance. Ignore the screens and just focus on the hosts and their questions. Keep eye contact with the hosts all of the time while delivering your answers.

> **PRO TIP: Use your best material first**
>
> Remember that old expression about saving the best until last? Don't do it. Broadcast interviews aren't rock concerts where the last song really brings the house down. In fact, you never really know the moment when a broadcast interview is going to end. There might be plans for the interview to go for 10 minutes, but it could get cut back to two minutes because of breaking news. If you have a great sound bite, or an important key message to share, you need to get to it early, preferably in your answer to the first or second question. Use the bounce technique (discussed later in this book) to politely get to your key messages if the need arises. This is true of all live interviews, whether for TV, radio or online.

Live TV at a remote studio

There are times when you will do live television interviews in a separate studio and never actually meet the hosts in person. This may be because you are located in a different city (you might live in Melbourne, but the program is broadcast from Sydney for example), or sometimes you might be in a studio in the same broadcast complex, but for one reason or another you are placed in a smaller studio.

In these situations, most of the advice for in-studio interviews still applies, but there are a few differences.

A technician will most likely give you an IFB (interruptible feedback) earpiece to wear. This is a small, unobtrusive earphone that will enable you to hear the questions that the hosts ask you. You'll feel like a secret service operative with your earpiece in! Sometimes a producer might talk to you over the earpiece, greet you and let you know how many minutes remain until the segment is on.

In these remote studio locations, you should look at the camera for the duration of the entire interview. Never look away! Not up, not down, not to the side. Always look at the camera! This includes while you are being asked questions, while someone else is speaking and while you are speaking. If there is a TV monitor below or near the camera showing yourself or the program hosts, don't be tempted to look at that monitor. Look into the camera barrel the entire time.

The reason you must keep looking at the camera the whole time, even when not talking, is that these interviews may go to air as a "split screen". This means you, the hosts and any other interviewees are shown in small boxes to viewers at home, all at the same time. So another interviewee might be asked a question, but we still see your face while they are answering. And while you are being asked a question, if you grimace or frown, the audience will see it. So be careful!

When the interview is finished, stay in your position and keep looking at the camera. You never know if the hosts may return to you for another quick comment, even when you feel the interview is over. The director will let you know via your earpiece when the interview has definitely wrapped up and you've been cleared to move.

One thing to be aware of with remote studios (and sometimes even in the big studios at major networks) is that using props usually won't work unless you've arranged it with the producer beforehand. In remote studios, the camera position is usually fixed, so if you hold something up, such as a book or newspaper, it may appear out of focus and look silly. If you want to use a prop, discuss it with the producer before your interview. If you're the author of a book, for example, it might be better to supply the producer with a digital image of its cover, rather than holding it up, not knowing if the audience will be able to see it clearly.

> **PRO TIP: Be careful around microphones**
>
> Many great careers have been sunk when people have said awkward things on microphone when they didn't think anyone was listening. TV studios are dangerous places. In fact, anywhere with microphones and cameras can be. Be aware that if you are wearing a microphone, many people in the broadcast complex, such as in the control room, will be able to hear what you are saying, and what you

> say might even be recorded, even if it is not actually broadcast to air. This isn't a deliberate tactic to catch you out, it's just standard practice to record the outputs from studios at all times. The importance of being careful around recording equipment is the same whether interviews are live or pre-recorded.

Live TV as a live-cross to you

Sometimes live interviews won't take place in a studio at all. "Live-crosses" follow the same principles as interviews in remote studios, but are conducted somewhere else. The location might be more convenient to you, or reflective of the story, such as an event location, at the scene of breaking news, at your home or at your offices.

Once upon a time, these crosses were facilitated by satellite link trucks, with several technicians, a producer, a sound recordist and a camera operator all coming to visit you. These days, it's not uncommon for a camera operator to come alone with a remote broadcast kit in a backpack. Technology has come a long way.

Give some consideration to where you will want to conduct the interview, and allow for some options that are a little quieter (not next to a noisy road for example). Feel free to suggest some options, but the camera operator will usually scout the area and choose the location that they know will be best. Their priority is making you look and sound good.

Don't be surprised if they ask to move some furniture to allow for the best shot.

The crew will need plenty of time to set up, and may arrive 45-60 minutes ahead of your interview time. The producer will establish all of these details when booking with you. The principles of a remote studio apply, and you will be given an IFB earpiece. You will usually be standing up, rather than sitting down. There is unlikely to be a monitor where you can see yourself or the hosts. Just like in a remote studio, you should keep eye contact with the camera the whole time.

> **PRO TIP: Great answers get a second life**
>
> Live-crosses on TV or radio can often give you multiple bites at the media cherry. What do I mean by this? Well, your interview might last several minutes when it is broadcast live-to-air on the program, but you might also find that a sentence or two from the interview gains a second life as a sound bite or news grab in a later news bulletin. This is especially true if it is a big story and your comments are memorable. This is all the more reason to pepper your responses in live interviews with memorable sound bites.

Live interviews in the age of Zoom

Skype, Zoom, FaceTime and other web-based technologies

have become increasingly common in use for remote interviews. During the COVID-19 pandemic, this became very prevalent, and we have since become accustomed to interviewees appearing on TV from their lounge rooms or home offices. If doing an interview using a web interface:

- It's absolutely essential to raise your computer's webcam or your smart phone to eye level, using books or boxes if necessary. If you leave your laptop down on the desk and look down toward your webcam, the audience will get a very unflattering view of you, right up your nose.

- Lighting is important. To be looking your best, you should have a light source in front of your face, rather than behind it. If there's a window in the room, face towards it, so that the natural light is falling on your face. Don't sit with your back to a window, because this will give you a silhouette-like appearance. You don't want people to think you're in witness protection, do you?

- If you want to take lighting to the next level, consider buying a ring light, or other form of light that will shine more light on your face. These lights can be set up and taken down easily, and can help eliminate any unsightly shadows on your face. They're available from camera stores, office goods retailers and many places online.

- Be aware of how your background looks. Is it clean? Are there distractions? Will people be trying to make out the names of the books on your bookshelves or will they be concentrating on what you say? Remember, you don't want anything behind you to distract from your key messages.

- Test your technology well in advance of your interview. Confirm which app the producers want to use for the cross to you and make sure that it's downloaded, updated and working properly. Don't leave this check until the last minute. You don't want to miss an interview because of a forgotten password or a missing plug-in!

- Maximising your available internet speed is also highly advised. WiFi can sometimes be a little unreliable, so if you have a ethernet network cable, consider plugging it into your modem or router to improve speed.

- Computer speed can also make a difference. You can improve speed by shutting down any unnecessary programs that might be using up memory and resources. Turning on-screen notifications off, will also help. Pop-up notifications during an interview can be awfully distracting for both yourself and the audience. Especially if they come with an audible ding!

- Avoid bulky overhead earphones. If you have access to some wireless or bluetooth earphones, try to use them for your interview as they are more discreet and less distracting than having cables dangling from your ears. You might also want to consider purchasing an external USB microphone if you're not satisfied with the quality of your computer's in-built microphone.

- Video quality matters. Some computers, even some Apple models, have very low-resolution webcams, so you might want to think about buying an external webcam to improve picture quality, or even using your mobile phone, as the camera quality on modern smartphones is often better than a webcam.

- Don't feel you have to do an interview from a certain part of your home or office just because that's where you usually use your computer. If there is a better location with better lighting or background, move your computer to this space for the duration of the interview. Make some effort to ensure that you and your environment are looking as good as possible.

- Keep looking into the camera the whole time. It can be hard to avoid looking at the computer monitor, especially if the interviewer's face is on it, but it's crucial that you keep looking into your webcam the whole time. Eye contact helps build a connection with the audience. By looking at your computer monitor instead of your webcam, it can appear as though you are looking away. To help remind you where to look, you may want to draw some arrows on bright sticky notes pointing to the camera.

PRO TIP: Avoid interruptions

Make sure you are in a space where you won't be interrupted, whether it's by other people, children, your pets, or a ringing telephone. You might be familiar with a BBC interview from a few years ago when the subject's children came marching in halfway through, derailing the entire interview. As funny as it was, you don't want this happening to you. When you have an opportunity to be interviewed, you want to be remembered for your key messages, not immortalised as a blooper on YouTube.

Live radio interviews

Live radio interviews can take place either in the studio, or remotely via telephone. These day most radio interviews are conducted by telephone, simply for convenience, as it's not always possible for interviewees to get to a studio. That said, radio stations do have guests in studios from time to time. When a producer books an interview with you, they will let you know which is preferred.

For radio studios, just like with in-studio TV appearances, make sure you give yourself plenty of time to arrive. A producer will usher you into the studio at your interview time, and you'll usually wear large studio headphones. You may be seated or standing, depending on the studio set-up.

A word of caution about radio studios is that these days,

many stations might also make video recordings of your interview. They may be broadcasting live via webcam or capturing video content for later release on social media. Be aware that you may need to be conscious of your actions and appearance, including your clothing and grooming, even though it's technically a radio interview.

If the interview is happening via phone rather than at a studio, make sure you organise yourself a quiet space where you are not going to be disturbed. Lock the door, and turn off anything that is likely to make a noise. Doing the interview on a landline rather than a mobile phone will mean it is less likely to drop out, so do this if possible to improve call quality.

Remember radio interviews can be cut short at any moment, so it's important to get to your best material very early in the interview. If you are on a radio program to promote a book, an event or launch, don't wait for a question from the interviewer about it. Get straight to it in one of your early answers as you may not get another opportunity.

A unique part of radio is that in addition to the interviewer asking you questions, sometimes listeners will be invited to call in to the show. Sometimes you'll know it in advance, but at other times the host might spring it on you. These calls might be straightforward and easily dealt with, or the callers might be angry or aggressive. Treat any caller with courtesy, respect and understanding. Remember, although you are talking to the caller, the whole audience is listening and judging you on what you say and how you say it. If you can't solve a problem for a listener on the spot, tell them you will have someone in your organisation contact them afterwards to make sure that their problem can be resolved.

> **PRO TIP: Give yourself a cheat sheet**
>
> If your interview is over the phone, whether it's for radio, print or online, there is no harm in having a single A4 page cheat sheet, with your key messages and any news grabs or important statistics, in large type, ready to refer to at any time if you get stuck. It's a bit like an acrobat having a trampoline hidden from the audience. Hopefully you don't need to use it, but it's there if you get stuck. Only use the cheat sheet in an emergency, don't just read off it for the sake of it. And remember you can only have a cheat sheet for interviews where the interviewer can't see you. For television, in a studio, or where you're in person with a reporter, forget about it! For these interviews, by all means create a cheat sheet and use it to study before an interview. Just don't bring it with you.

Pre-recorded TV interviews

Nightly news

Most pre-recorded TV interviews for the nightly news have a key purpose for the reporter: getting clear sound bites. Because their stories are quite short, they are really only looking for and listening out for one or two really memorable sound bites that will stand out in their report.

For this reason, it's important to come armed with sound bites or news grabs to pepper through your responses. You'll also need to make sure your answers are short, sharp, and to-the-point. If you share memorable sound bites, the audience is much more likely to connect with your key messages.

In these pre-recorded interviews it's also really important to answer in full sentences and incorporate part of the question in your answer in order to give your answers some context.

So, if you're asked:

> "What's the best part of living in Australia?"

Your answer shouldn't be:

> "The golden beaches."

Instead, it should be:

> "The best part of living in Australia is the golden beaches."

Why do this? The principal reason is that the reporter's question will not make it to air, only your answers will, so you need to give the answer some context so it is usable in the final broadcast.

There is one exception to this rule about encapsulating the question in the answer, and that's where the question has contained a negative inference. You don't want to repeat back a negative inference as part of a denial. We all remember, for example, Richard Nixon saying "I'm not a crook". So how do you deal with negative inferences in questions? Don't worry, we'll get to that in a later chapter.

Don't feel dejected with the knowledge that the reporter will only use a couple of sound bites in the final story even though they spent a long time interviewing you. Everything else you say still matters, and will help give the reporter more background to help them understand the story. You will find they will paraphrase some of what you say in their own words in their voiceover.

If you make a mistake in these pre-recorded interviews by losing your train of thought, or stumbling or stammering, you can easily make a quick recovery by stopping and starting again. The reporter will usually be glad you did, because it will give them a second, clearer version, that they will be able to use in their report.

To do this, stop your sentence completely and say "actually just let me rephrase that", and start it from the beginning again. It means you will deliver a nice, clean news grab for a reporter, who will be grateful to be able to use it in their story. Remember this technique of restarting your answer is only really available to you in pre-recorded interviews.

For pre-recorded interviews, you could be seated in a chair, or standing up. It all depends on the context and style of the story. At other times, you might even be walking alongside the reporter and talking to them, or you might be demonstrating a product to them. Almost always, your eye contact should be on the reporter. If in doubt, check with the reporter where they would like you to be looking.

> **PRO TIP: Never, ever waste an answer**
>
> At the end of most pre-recorded interviews, the reporter may give you the opportunity for a final thought. Usually they'll say, "is there anything else you want to add?" or words to that effect. I know it can be tempting to say no so that you can hot-foot it out of there, but the answer to this question is always, always, always yes. It's the ultimate gimme. If, up to this point, the interviewer hasn't asked a question that easily lent itself to delivering one of your key messages, then this is a perfect chance to get that message across. It's a free kick! Even if you feel the interview has gone well, this is still another chance to repeat one of those messages. Another reason this final answer is so important is that because it's the last thing you say, it will most likely stick in the reporter's mind.

Investigative programs

Pre-recorded interviews for longer form or investigative programs are a little different. Instead of going for just a few minutes, with the reporter listening out for key news grabs, investigative interviews are far more probing and could go for an hour or even more. The principles are largely the same as other pre-recorded interviews but the journalist is seeking more information or perspective than a reporter preparing a short story for the nightly news.

> **PRO TIP: Don't be afraid of silence**
>
> Some of the best interviewers will use moments of pause or silence in order to make things awkward and perhaps lead you to add additional information that you hadn't planned on providing. As human beings we have a tendency to fill silence with our own words. But don't be lured into this trap. Don't be afraid of silence. And if you absolutely must fill the vacuum with something, make sure it's one of your key messages.

Radio newsroom interviews

From time to time, a radio newsroom might contact you (or your communications team will contact them), to supply them with some audio sound bites or news grabs for a radio news bulletin. An interview with a journalist from a radio newsroom will be different to the interviews you hear live-to-air during a talkback program.

Radio newsroom interviews don't go live-to-air. Instead, they are used by the newsroom to include a short snippet of your voice as a sound bite in the hourly news bulletin. These are conducted over the phone and the journalist will be looking for short, sharp, memorable pieces of audio that will make an impact in their bulletin. The interviews usually last only a few minutes. The questions will usually be very straightforward, but don't be surprised if you get a curly one or two.

If you're asked to phone a radio newsroom, it's best to call at about a quarter past the hour. Calling right on the hour or half-hour (or just before), means you've likely called when a journalist is just about to read the news (or actually reading it!) and is unable to take your call. Even calling a few minutes before news time is a big no-no. If a radio journalist does pick up the phone at this time, they're likely to be very short with you and you may damage your relationship with them.

> **PRO TIP: Stop talking when you finish your answer**
>
> When you say too much, you risk diluting your messages. Over-answering could also get you into trouble, because the more you say, the more you risk saying something you hadn't intended to. Keep your answers concise; two or three sentences at most. If the reporter wants additional detail or clarification, they will ask you for it.

Over the phone with an online or print reporter

Print and online reporters are usually so busy that most of their interviews will be conducted over the phone. The same principles for pre-recorded broadcast interviews generally apply with these interviews too. Reporters are likely to either type out your responses, or make an audio recording of the interview so that they can listen back to it again and choose some of your quotes to use in the story. They will usually tell you if you are being recorded, but you should always assume they are recording anyway.

Like broadcast interviewers listening for sound bites, these reporters will be keenly listening for you to deliver really quotable quotes that will make an impact in the story. If you hear them typing ferociously in one particular section, you might even slow down or repeat your point. It's usually because they found what you said interesting or noteworthy.

Because these interviews are conducted over the phone, you can have a cheat sheet handy with your key messages, quotable quotes and any statistics or data that you might need to reference. At the end of this interview, take the opportunity to really hammer home one of your key messages before you hang up.

In person with an online or print reporter

If you're doing an in-person interview with an online or print reporter, most of the principles from above apply. One word of warning though, if you're in a casual setting, you shouldn't let your guard down. Sometimes in-person interviews might occur in a bar, a café, or even over lunch or dinner. It's easy to lose a sense of perspective in these situations when you become too relaxed and say too much, or embarrassingly reveal more than you intended. Don't believe for a moment when the reporter tells you that "you're just having a friendly chat". Consider everything you say to be on the record and quotable, and don't ever get too comfortable.

A press conference

A press conference (also called media conference, a "presser", "all-in", or "doorstop" in industry terminology), is a different style of interview altogether. In these situations, you will face a group of journalists, along with camera operators and photographers in one big group, rather than dealing with one-on-one interviews.

Press conferences are an efficient way to get a message to a large group of journalists all at once, at times when it would be practically or logistically impossible to grant interviews to them individually. They're used commonly by politicians, emergency services and sporting teams but also by other spokespeople when the situation demands it, such as breaking news, major announcements or launches.

The advent of cable television and live-streaming on the internet has meant that many media conferences, once only attended by the press, can be viewed live by the general public. This means the media conference actually serves two purposes: the initial broadcast, when it is broadcast raw in its entirety, and then again when it is repurposed later in the day with excerpts or quotes included in news stories, reports and packages.

Media conferences traditionally start with a spokesperson making a comment or statement (usually a discussion or summary of their key messages) and then inviting journalists to ask any questions that they wish.

It should be obvious that you wouldn't hold a press conference without excellent communications support: a team or consultant to work with reporters, distribute your media release, scope the setting, call for the last question if things are going on too long and deal with any follow up issues once the spokesperson has departed.

Fronting a media conference can be quite daunting because of the rows of TV cameras, big lights, photographer's flashes and reporters barking questions. Knowing the logistics, such as where you will be standing or sitting, and having a rehearsal in advance will help boost your confidence. Also, make sure you know where the exit is so you can make a speedy departure when it is time to leave.

When it comes to questions, reporters may try to scream over the top of each other. If you haven't heard a question clearly, it's OK to ask the reporter to repeat it. Deal slowly and methodically with each question. In terms of eye contact, it's usually best to look straight ahead at all times so that all of the cameras will have a good view of you. It's not necessary to look the reporters in the eye as you answer their questions, especially if this means turning side on.

Before calling a media conference, it's worth discussing with your communications team or consultant whether it's the best way to get your message across. In times of crisis, your time may be limited. If you will only be able to take a couple of questions (because you need to get back to an operations centre during a breaking news event for example), let this be known at the outset.

> **PRO TIP: Count down the questions and finish**
>
> You don't want a media conference to either be so short that you get accused of avoiding questions, or so long that you risk diluting your key messages. A technique to wrap things up once questions become repetitive is to indicate that you'll take just three more, gesturing to the three reporters whose questions you'll answer. Once you've answered their questions, thank everyone for their time, promise you will give another update soon and make for the exit. Don't look back, even if reporters are still calling questions at you. Oh, and make sure you know where the exit is first!

An ambush interview

An ambush occurs when a journalist confronts you without notice and starts asking you questions on the spot. It is a common technique used by tabloid and investigative television programs. Reporters might use this tactic when you have repeatedly refused an interview, or they may spring it on you if they deliberately want to capture a surprised reaction, when they know that you don't expect to see them. Journalists should know that they can't trespass onto private or company property, so ambushes (which some media outlets refer to as "bounces"), usually occur in public places, streets, parks and carparks. A reporter, photographer or camera crew may surveil you for some time to know when you are likely to be in a particular place before pouncing.

An ambush can be upsetting and unexpected, but it is worth giving some consideration in advance to what you would do if you were ever to find yourself in such a situation. If you avoid questions, shove the camera operator and tell them "get out of my face", it can be a very bad look. A more sensible approach is to stop, tell the reporter with sincerity that you are happy to be interviewed, but that it would be more appropriate to do it properly by sitting down together for a formal interview at a later stage. Give them your card, and say that you're more than happy to set up a time for a discussion in a setting where you can give their important questions the time they deserve, even later that same day if they wish. Doing so means that you won't appear defensive or obstructive with the reporter and it also buys you time to prepare for the interview. Believe me, the reporter is hoping you push the camera and run away. If you do, it's the shot that will run on the promo for their show. Don't give them that shot.

Ambushes are often the climax of a situation where an interviewee has continually rebuffed formal interview requests by email or phone, over and over again. If your strategy has been to avoid questioning, by ignoring requests, or simply releasing written statements, an ambush is a tactic that some journalists might employ to try to finally get some answers.

> **PRO TIP: Don't touch the camera.**
>
> Ever. You'll look violent and aggressive. Whatever you do, don't do it.

Interview by email

In this day and age, busy print and online reporters are often pressed for time. Instead of asking for an interview over the phone, they might be happy to email you a list of questions, and have you email your responses in return. It really just depends on the type of story they are working on.

An argument in favour of giving an email interview is that you have a little more time to think about the questions and edit your answers to ensure they are direct, concise and accurate. You can proofread them to make sure you haven't said anything wrong.

But simply emailing your responses can make it difficult to build a rapport with the reporter. Emails often lack the warmth of a genuine conversation, and it can be difficult to convey tone, nuance and additional context in your answers.

If a reporter offers you an email interview, let them know you are happy to respond by email if they wish, but that you're also more than happy to speak to them on the phone too, if they have the time. Give them the choice. When you submit your email answers, make sure you also include your phone number and let them know you're willing to follow up any additional questions they have.

Most importantly, don't fire off any emails before checking your responses with your communications team or consultant first.

> **PRO TIP: Be cautious about just "releasing a statement"**
>
> It's commonplace for organisations to release a written statement, rather than consenting to an interview, particularly when the subject matter is controversial. Organisations do it so that they can appear to be responding to the story, without having a spokesperson deal with difficult questions. But beware. Astute reporters will make it clear in their reports that you wouldn't agree to an interview and "hid" behind a statement. Written statements aren't necessarily an easy way out. They often lack nuance and tone, and raise more questions than they answer. There's no reason a confident, competent, media-trained spokesperson shouldn't agree to be interviewed, unless some legal or logistical issue prevents them from doing so.

11.

HANDLING TOUGH QUESTIONS

What are they going to ask?

Not knowing what the questions will be is often the greatest source of anxiety prior to an interview. Senior executives are used to being in control nearly all of the time, but a media interview is one of those rare occasions where they cede control to someone else. They spend time worrying about what they'll be asked, whether they'll be caught out and whether their answers might embarrass their company.

One of the single most important pieces of advice I can give for handling media interviews is to remind you that *you* are in control of absolutely everything you say. This is *your* interview. Sure, you can't choose the questions, but you absolutely choose every single answer you give. You choose what you say and how much you say. And you also choose how much you engage with negative questions. It's *your* voice and they're *your* words. It might not feel like it, but every interview is in your control, not the journalist's.

How do you stay in control? Read on and find out.

The driver's seat

Before we get to a practical framework that you can use for handling difficult questions, I want to spend some time dealing with the psychology of an interview and the power dynamics involved.

It's easy to see why an interviewee might feel powerless against a journalist. The perceived power imbalance starts with the environment of the interview. As a guest, the unfamiliar setting, with cameras, bright lights and microphones can feel awfully intimidating.

For the reporter, it's not intimidating at all. It's their home turf. You're there as a guest, but it's their workplace and they're in it every day. It's easy to get carried away and think it's the interviewer's show. Their newspaper. Their website. Their podcast. And you're just a guest who is lucky to be in their presence.

Wrong.

This is *your* interview. You are volunteering *your* time and giving *your* answers. No one can force you to say anything. Shifting your perspective is empowering. If you do so, you put yourself in the driver's seat. The reporter will ask the questions that they want. But it's you who is steering the interview in the direction you want it to go. The challenge is to do so professionally and courteously, in a way that doesn't appear obstrutive, evasive or combative.

The best approach

There is nothing more frustrating than watching an interviewee deliberately and obviously avoid a question. Politicians are a group who frequently fall into this category and my view is that there is often a net worse effect on them as a result of choosing to so obviously avoid questions. Audiences can spot it a mile away, and a good interviewer will call them out on it and make it clear they haven't answered the question. Viewers may well form a judgment that the interviewee can't be trusted because of how blatantly they tried to avoid questions.

My advice is that you should answer every question in at least some form, or it will be very obvious to both the interviewer and their audience that you are being evasive. What is critical is how much time in your response you spend dealing with the difficult or negative part of the question. The best approach is, at the very least, to give a cursory response to any negativity raised in the question and move on to your key messages as quickly as possible. I call this technique, the bounce technique.

The bounce technique

The bounce technique helps you bounce away from a difficult line of questioning, to an area that you're more comfortable talking about. It's a technique that keeps you in control. If it was a normal conversation with a friend, you might think of it as "politely changing the subject". But remember, it's critical that you at least address the question at the beginning of your answer, otherwise you will be accused of avoiding it entirely.

If we represent a full response, using the bounce technique, as a flowchart, it looks like this:

Short Answer

↓

Bounce Statement

↓

Key Message

An example in practice

Let's imagine a scenario where a private health fund has increased its membership fees by 10%. The CEO is giving a wide-ranging interview to a reporter about the future of the company, and until now, the interview has covered mostly positive territory for the business. But the reporter changes tack, and asks a more pointed question:

> *"Your membership fees are through the roof. You're really ripping people off now aren't you?"*

A bad response from the CEO would be to treat the question as a personal attack, react strongly and reiterate the negativity of the question in their response:

> "*I was told this was going to be a positive interview. We don't rip anyone off. Prices go up sometimes, that's how the world works. Now your next question ought to be about something else, otherwise this interview is over.*"

The gruff response isn't helpful. The CEO might think he has showed the reporter who the boss is, but the audience will judge them as being aggressive and angry. It's a very poor look for the company.

But what if the CEO tried a different response?

> "*No, that's not the case. What our members need to know is that their fees cover more treatment than any other insurer, and they can always call us to change their level of cover, because what we want is for everyone to have the most appropriate policy for their family.*"

This is a much better response. It dealt directly with the negative inference in the question, with a short answer, saying "No, that's not the case". It then included a bounce statement which was, "what our members need to know is", before moving onto the key message, which was information about the flexibility of the company's policies.

Short Answer:
"No that's not the case…"

↓

Bounce Statement:
"…what our members need to know is…"

↓

Key Message:
"…that their fees cover more treatment than any other

insurer, and they can always call us to change their level of cover, because what we want is for everyone to have the most appropriate policy for their family."

In the response above, the CEO didn't avoid the question altogether, even though it was a difficult one. They answered it very briefly, used a bounce statement to move the subject on, then spent about 90% of their response time on a key message.

Some handy ways to bounce

There are plenty of bounce statements that you can weave through your responses. Here are some commonly used ones:

- "What's important to remember though…"
- "What our members are telling us however…"
- "What our research is showing us…"
- "What we don't want people to forget is…"
- "But what's also important here is…"
- "But what I am focusing on at the moment is…"
- "But what we can't lose sight of is…"
- "At the end of the day, what's important is…
- "What I'm more excited about is…"
- "What people are really talking about is…"

The more you say, the more they can quote you on

Remember, the longer you spend talking about the negative aspects of a question, the more negative material you give the reporter to quote you on. The less you say, the less they can use. Remember earlier in the book when we talked about the importance of having a goal? I bet wasting valuable minutes of an interview talking about negative material was not your goal.

This is why using the bounce technique is so important. When you use this technique you move the conversation to topic areas and messages that you are more confident talking about. Of course, there is no guarantee that if you use the bounce technique, a reporter won't follow-up with another question that tries to draw you into talking about the negative topic. That's their job. Your job is to use the bounce technique again so that you can speak about your key messages instead.

Remember, you can't choose the questions, but you always choose your answers! The power is all yours.

Have the "short answers" ready

In some circumstances, you'll know before an interview that some negative questions are coming and the audience will expect you to respond to them. So it's important to have the "short answers" for these tricky issues prepared in advance, so you're ready to deliver them in the interview, and not caught on the hop.

Getting ready for these difficult questions in advance may

well be the most important part of your preparation. It's pretty rare that a difficult question will blindside you entirely, so there is no excuse for not considering in advance the potential weak spots, problem areas and common issues faced by your organisation and how you plan to address them. A well prepared organisation will have a document containing standard short responses to predictable issues, which any interviewee can refer to as part of their preparation. If yours doesn't have one, I'd recommend starting to prepare it soon.

What's important when it comes to answering the difficult questions is keeping your "short answer" part of your response exactly that: concise, direct and simple. Sometimes it might be a single word: yes or no. Sometimes it might be a couple of sentences. But once you've given your short answer, it's crucial that you move the discussion on to your key message.

But it's not just for difficult questions

The bounce technique is handy for more than just difficult questions. Sometimes you might be asked questions that are off-track, irrelevant, or not quite what you'd hoped to talk about. This might not be intentional on the behalf of the reporter. It may be that they aren't an expert in the subject and so you must take the initiative to drive the discussion to other topics.

You can use the bounce technique to subtly, politely and courteously redirect the discussion. Let's imagine a scenario where a musician wants to talk about their new album, but the reporter keeps asking about a rumoured romance instead, after a tabloid newspaper published photos of the musician on a beach with a new lover.

The reporter's question goes something like this:

> "You've been single for quite a few years now, but everyone is talking about the photos of you in Fiji with a special someone. Can we safely say you're off the market right now?"

The musician might be upset to have been asked this question, wants to keep their private life private, and wants to talk about their album instead.

A bad way of venting this frustration might be to say:

> "My publicist told you not ask any personal questions. You should be ashamed of yourself."

A more effective response to move the conversation back to the new album might be:

> "Where would we be without gossip magazines hey! But you know, I'm very private with that stuff, and my fans know that too. My focus is really on the album because it's our first new material in three years. The big news today is that we're touring as well, and it's going to be stadium shows in every capital city. My passion has always been the big gigs, and I'm super excited to hear what our fans think of the album."

Easily done. The discussion was tactfully moved on from

romance questions and the musician got in a big plug for their album and tour. That's a win.

It's your job to get your messages across

At the end of an interview, it's not uncommon for a frustrated interviewee to be upset, saying "I can't believe the reporter didn't ask any questions about [insert prepared topic here]".

The truth is, the responsibility to talk about the prepared topic was theirs. In the example above, the questions might not have been about the musician's album. But the onus was on the musician to take control of the interview politely, and use a bounce technique to get them to the safer territory that they did want to talk about.

What if the question is beyond your area of expertise?

Sometimes you might be asked questions outside your area of responsibility in your organisation, or beyond your knowledge or expertise. How do you deal with that? Politely, courteously, and again by using the bounce technique.

Let's imagine, for example, that the health minister is cutting the ribbon at the opening of a new hospital. But on the same day, there have been massive commuter delays on the city's train lines. As a member of the government, it's inevitable that the health minister will be asked about the problem, even though it's outside their direct portfolio.

So if a reporter asks:

> *"Is the government embarrassed that trains aren't running on time?"*

A good answer for the health minister might be:

> *"Look, the transport minister has commented on that today and made the point that the timetables will be examined….but can I just say, my focus today as health minister, is the great sense of pride that comes with opening this new hospital that will provide much needed service for residents in this area. The hospital is meeting the health needs of the region as well as creating a thousand new jobs."*

Notice that the answer politely acknowledges the question is a valid one, but that commentary on it should be made by the relevant minister. The health minister then bounces away, "can I just say, my focus today as health minister is…" and then continues with key messaging in relation to the hospital topic.

Sometimes reporters will absolutely know that you're not equipped or authorised to comment on a particular issue or topic, but they will give it a go anyway. It's your job to stay in control and bounce away from the problematic area. Note that you should never say "I can't comment on that", or "I'm not authorised to speak about that". Technically that might be true, but it makes you appear evasive. There's always something you can say. That's why we have key messages prepared and ready to deliver.

Let's imagine a football player is at a post-match press conference, and is asked about an off-field controversy involving a sponsor. Commentary on the issue is best handled by the CEO, so how can the player deal with it when it comes up?

If the reporter asks:

> *"Are you concerned that the club's image is suffering as a result of the revelations about X sponsor this week"*

A good way to respond might be:

> *"I know that's a major issue and is being handled by the club leadership at the moment. As a player, all of my energy this week went into tonight's match. I'm really pleased that I didn't have any problems with my knee out there, and I know that tonight's win will fill all of us with confidence going into the semi-finals."*

And if the reporter presses again:

> *"But the sponsorship thing has been a big one this week, surely you've got an opinion on how it should be handled"*

It's important the player keeps using the bounce technique:

> *"As I said, the issue is very much in the hands of club leadership. What our fans want is for us to be a strong force in the semi-finals, so our focus as a playing group needs to be on our consistency of play and that's why we're so pleased with the result tonight, and we're looking forward to the build-up ahead of next week."*

I don't know that…but I do know this!

There will be times when you're asked a question, but just can't recall the answer. It might be on the tip of your tongue, but you've just gone blank. Or it might be a request for a fact or figure that you just don't know. We're all fallible, and within reason, audiences are likely to accept your momentary lack of knowledge if you are authentic and humble about it. If you get stuck, the best solution is to acknowledge that the question is an important one, and that you'll commit to getting the relevant details to the reporter as soon as possible after the interview. Then use the bounce technique to move on to other prepared material that you do know more about.

For example, let's imagine the director of the education department is answering questions in a radio interview about a group of students who've been arrested after allegedly selling drugs on school premises. The host asks this question:

> *"Exactly how many students were arrested?"*

But the director's mind goes blank. Was it four, five, six or seven? The director can't remember! An ineffective response would be:

> *"I'm not sure off the top of my head. That number hasn't been given to me."*

A more effective response would be:

> *"It was several students. We'll be able to confirm the*

> *precise number for your listeners shortly, but let me say this more broadly: even one arrest is one too many. On this issue as a whole, we're totally committed to the safety and wellbeing of students in our schools, and we'll continue to investigate what processes can be improved to make that happen."*

Notice in this response, the interviewee didn't know the correct number, but didn't show any embarrassment about it. More importantly, they got a key message about safety and wellbeing across, which in the scheme of things, was more important.

What if you're asked to speculate?

Sometimes you will be asked questions where an outcome or result isn't known yet. You might be encouraged to speculate if asked a hypothetical question by a reporter. But you shouldn't engage in speculation because your answers could come back to haunt you.

When a reporter asks you to speculate, or if their question contains a premise that might not be true, we use a technique to respond called reframing.

Imagine the treasurer gets asked a question about what they will do if a new policy fails. The question might be:

> *"If the stimulus package doesn't do anything to turn around unemployment, will you consider an additional range of incentive measures to boost the economy?"*

The question is a hypothetical one and is predicated on

a presumption of failure. An ineffective response to this would be:

> *"I'm not going to be caught up in hypotheticals. They're a waste of time."*

Some politicians commonly use language such as:

> *"I don't agree with the premise of your question."*

It's true that as an interviewee, you don't need to speculate and that sometimes reporters will ask questions with a faulty premise.

A good approach would be to respond in this way:

> *"It's important that we don't speculate on any outcomes. The wisest course of action is for us to fully implement the stimulus package, keeping in mind that it offers a fantastic deal for workers and employers and we are absolutely confident that it will deliver strong outcomes for hard working Australians."*

What if you get asked about a competitor?

Questions about your competitors and adversaries should be answered with caution and discretion. In some industries, especially politics, interviewees relish the chance to talk about their opponents and highlight their flaws. For most others though, it's good advice that that unless it is absolutely necessary to comment, the less you say about your competitors, the better. Think of it from the audience's perspective. Will it really help your image if you are running your opponents into the ground or saying negative things about them?

More importantly, why would you waste any valuable time at all in an interview talking about others, when you could be talking about yourself? Once again here, the bounce technique is your friend.

Imagine the CEO of a shoe company being asked about a drop in sales by a competitor, after a big product launch of theirs was a flop in the market. The CEO might get asked:

> *"Why do you think people aren't buying X shoes anymore?"*

The question is a bit of a trap to get the CEO to criticise their rivals. An effective way to handle this question might be:

> *"Oh look that's very much a matter for them. Our focus is always on delivering the right styles for our customers and we're really excited about the launch of our new winter range. I always say, 'if the shoe fits, wear it', and our customers take the same attitude, which is why our previous season releases sold out in just three days."*

Had the CEO spent time sticking the boot into the opposition, they'd have appeared aggressive. Instead the CEO used the bounce technique to drive the conversation back to their own business, and even threw in a sound bite for good measure.

Relax

This entire chapter has been devoted to handling difficult questions, but I certainly don't want to scare you off agreeing to interviews.

Don't assume every interview will be adversarial and full of tough questions with the reporter trying to catch you out. Many of the interviews you participate in will be straightforward, with the questions likely to be on topics you've prepared, offering great opportunities to share key messages. Remember, many reporters won't necessarily have detailed knowledge of your subject matter, so if they ask an off-topic question, they're probably not trying to catch you out, it might be that they just don't understand the topic as well as you do.

12.

MORE THAN WORDS

What makes a good spokesperson?

Good spokespeople are good communicators. They are talented at getting a message across and telling a story. For some people, communication skills come more naturally than for others. But don't worry, I'm of the firm view that communication skills can be developed and grown because they're all based on some basic key principles. People who grow to become excellent spokespeople all share some key skills. They've all got the C-Word, or more accurately, C-Words, plural. Good spokespeople are confident, calm, composed, concise and clear communicators, who have cut-through.

Let's start with confidence. Confidence doesn't mean having a big ego. In fact, when it comes to media interviews, ego can do more harm than good. Audiences can detect an annoyingly large ego and they don't respond well to it. The most genuinely confident people are authentic, warm and humble. Confidence comes from knowing your material intimately and being able to deliver it well. It comes from practicing over and over again, and from reminding yourself that you have the tools, framework and knowledge to give a great interview. Confidence comes from knowing you are equipped to handle difficult and unexpected questions.

A good spokesperson is a calm and composed spokesperson. They don't fly off the handle and they have a disposition that allows them to stay cool and collected, even during a crisis. They are a person who isn't phased by different personalities, such as those of belligerent or angry interviewers. They gather all the facts first and act carefully based on them. They're someone who can modify their response as a situation changes and whose own sense of ease relaxes others. A composed spokesperson isn't rattled by anything. They can handle technical problems with a good sense of humour or adapt to an interview being cut short due to breaking news. And they do it all with a smile.

Why is being concise important? One of the challenges that all spokespeople face is the need to compress a plethora of complex information into just a few short words or sentences. Strong spokespeople can do that, because they have the ability to filter out what isn't important to an audience and only share what is. Good spokespeople know that only a small amount of what they say in an interview will be used in the final story, so they learn to speak with impact. Part of that impact comes from being concise, direct and to the point.

When a good spokesperson has given an interview, their points of view and the information they share are abundantly clear to their audience. No one is left in any doubt. This clarity of communication often comes from the words they have chosen to use. Clear spokespeople use straightforward terms and don't cloud any of their messages with unnecessary detail, which could interfere with achieving their overall goal.

And finally, a good spokesperson is one who can cut through the noise, so that people listen. Because we all get bombarded with hundreds of messages every single day, smart spokespeople know how to deliver a message in a way that will ensure people pay attention. The cut-through of a good spokesperson comes because they are compelling and memorable.

The most exciting thing about developing the traits of a good spokesperson is that once they become familiar to you, they'll be valuable in almost every aspect of your life. If you can grow and develop these communication skills, you'll see improvements in many parts of your business and personal life, way beyond their use in media interviews alone. Being a good communicator will set you apart from the pack.

Who should be our media spokesperson?

Appointing a spokesperson depends on the intended audience, and the goal that your organisation has for the interview.

Make no mistake. Whoever is at the very top of your organisation should be equipped, trained and ready to handle media interviews at short notice. A smart organisation ensures that their entire executive team is media trained and familiar with concepts such as key messaging and sound bites. All members of the team should have experience at handling difficult questions, and be competent at appearing on camera, should the need arise.

But that doesn't mean that the CEO, or even a member of the senior leadership should be the one doing every single interview. As an organisation, there will be times when your goal or messages might be better delivered by another member of the team. For a large tech company, for example, the CFO might be the best person with the most knowledge and experience to handle interviews with the business press, but not the right person to handle in-depth questions about the speed of the company's data servers and compliance policies. A technology specialist, who is a strong communicator, though being lower down the company's hierarchy, might be the perfect choice for that particular interview.

Clever companies know that it is helpful to encourage all of their staff to build their communication skills, regardless of their roles. Not all of these employees will be required to act as media spokespeople, but empowering them to speak memorably, deliver messages effectively and keep calm under pressure will give them crucial skills with value right across the workplace, not just for media interviews.

It's not just what you say

Until now in this book, much of our focus has been on *what* we say in interviews. But when it comes to communicating a message, many factors other than just the words we choose can influence how that message comes across. Our voice, gestures, posture, presentation, clothing and grooming must all match the tone we are trying to convey.

Get the look

Clothing is particularly important in visual mediums like television and online video. Your clothing should convey your intended tone and match your role in your organisation. Most importantly it should contribute to, and never distract from, your key messages. If a personal trainer is doing an interview, active wear is more than acceptable, in fact it's probably encouraged. A CEO in lycra though? Maybe not.

Patterned clothing

There are a few words of caution when it comes to clothing for television. I would always avoid fine stripes and checked patterns. These patterns can sometimes cause a strobing or shimmering effect on camera. Bold block colours come across a lot better than patterns and pastels, and they convey more authority. For suits and ties, heavy patterns or pin stripes can also be distracting. Wearing all white can be problematic too, so try contrasting a white shirt or blouse with a darker jacket. This is because white has a tendency to reflect light. Shiny materials should also be avoided for the same reasons.

Green should never be seen

When doing television interviews in a studio, there's a chance you might be sat in front of what is known as a green screen. These screens are used for projecting graphics and backdrops, and the risk is that if you are wearing the same colour as the screen, you may disappear into it. It will be as if you are wearing Harry Potter's invisibility cloak! Green screens are less common in modern TV studios, which tend to use plasma and LED screens for graphics, but to be on the safe side, I would avoid green regardless.

Keep it clean

It ought to go without saying that our clothing should be neat, presentable, and above all clean! But there are also times that we pull on an outfit, forgetting that we meant to take it to the dry cleaner after that incident with the spaghetti sauce a week ago. It's difficult to hide scuffs and stains on high-definition television. If you have an important interview later in the day, consider keeping your outfit on a hanger and changing into it just before your interview. You don't want the stress of trying to hide a coffee spill from a white shirt just before an interview. As well as being clean, your clothing should be ironed or pressed, if necessary. Avoid crumpled and creased clothes.

A good fit

It's important to make sure that whatever you are wearing fits properly. Remember, this is your moment in the spotlight, so you really want your clothing to flatter you, regardless of your size and shape. Like Goldilocks, you want your clothing not too big and not too small, you want it just right. If you've shifted sizes recently, consider shopping for a more flattering outfit, or borrowing some better fitting clothes from a helpful friend or colleague.

The waist down

We're used to the stereotyped caricature of a newsreader wearing a suit from the waist up and boardshorts down below. The truth is, if you're appearing on television, you never know where the shot is going to be cropped, and whether your legs will be visible. On some sets, you'll be seated behind a desk, on a couch or perched on a stool, so it's important to come dressed for any eventuality. Remember your entire outfit, including your shoes, might be visible to the audience. Take this into consideration when considering the length of your trousers or your hemline. And make sure your socks match!

Jewellery

Avoid noisy or distracting jewellery. A bracelet or bangle can look lovely but there's nothing worse than hearing it jingle as you move your hands or clunking on the desk. It's amazing how much noise studio microphones can pick up. Any jewellery that is too over the top can also be a visual distraction from your message. As lovely as your favourite enormous brooch that was passed down from your grandma is, if it's too big or bright, you risk the audience paying more attention to it, than what you are saying.

Make-up

Some TV studios will do your make-up for you before you appear on set, but this is not always the case. Make sure you check with the producer in advance.

The bright lights used in television and the sharp resolution of our modern televisions at home can accentuate all of our best and worst features. Make-up can even and smooth our complexion, remove the dark circles under our eyes, and ensure that we don't form beads of sweat on our forehead or a sheen on our cheeks, when we're under the harsh, hot lights of the studio.

For both ladies and gents, if you are going to do a lot of appearances on TV or video, I would encourage you to seek professional advice on the right products, tones and colours for you. The cosmetic counters at large department stores should be able to help you with this, and give you a lesson in applying the make-up if you haven't used it before. Let them know you're looking for make-up for TV, rather than everyday use. Keep in mind that interviews won't always be conducted in a studio. A reporter may visit you at your home or office, so being confident in applying your own make-up and styling your own hair is important.

Glasses

If it's possible to remove your prescription spectacles for an interview, it may be for the best. The reason for this is that the bright lights often used in interview settings can cause harsh reflections on the glass, and we will see white rectangular reflections on your glasses, rather than the colour of your eyes. Even on webcam interviews from home, the light from your computer monitor can reflect on your glasses making for a disturbing effect. If you absolutely must wear your glasses, that's OK. But if you can get away with not wearing them (if they are mostly for reading, for example), then it's best to go without.

Hats and sunglasses

Unless being a rockstar is a cornerstone of your personal brand, remove your sunglasses, even if the interview is outdoors. There are also very few reasons that you should wear a cap or hat in an interview (one of them might be that a sponsor is paying you millions of dollars to do it). But even for sporting stars, the peak of a cap or hat can cast nasty and unflattering shadows across your face. Avoid, if possible.

Last-minute checks

Before you appear on screen, do a last-minute "once-over". If you're wearing a tie, check it is straight. Make sure the zip of your trousers is done up. Make sure all your buttons are correctly fastened. Check your hair and your make-up. Dandruff on your shoulders? Brush it off. Lipstick on your teeth? Double-check for it! You can do all of these checks using a mirror or the selfie mode of your smart phone. If available, have a friend or colleague also double-check your appearance and let you know if anything needs fixing. Don't leave anything at all to chance.

Also, if you're headed to an interview, it's always a good idea to keep some essentials handy: think tissues, a bottle of water and emergency make-up. There is nothing worse than a dry mouth at the last minute, or a sniffle that just won't go away.

Using your voice

Our voices are absolutely crucial to the delivery of key messages, especially in broadcast interviews. The voice is perhaps the most powerful tool we have in conveying tone. A strong voice projects authority. A warm voice conveys authenticity. Your voice is unique to you, and it can help you put your own memorable stamp on an interview and set you apart from others. The use of your voice is particularly important in radio interviews and podcasts. When body language and facial expressions can't be seen, your voice is critical.

Some people seek out professional voice coaches to help refine the way they speak, but I don't think this is always necessary. The best advice I can give here is to embrace your own voice. It's the real you. You should strive for a natural, conversational delivery. Don't try to imitate someone else, or attempt to "put on" a professional sounding voice. Be yourself. If you try to sound like something, or someone that you're not, the audience will notice.

Tone

The tone your voice takes should reflect the overall goal of the interview and the message you are trying to share. If you're a CEO making an apology for the way your company has conducted itself, your tone needs to be remorseful and come from the heart. It must have a very human element and it can't be robotic. What's the point of an apology if it doesn't sound like you actually mean it?

But our tone needs to vary. Conveying specific information in an emergency, for example, means that your tone needs to be cool, controlled and match the gravity of the event without leading to panic.

And if you're announcing something fun, happy or that you're proud of, your tone should match that too. I've sat with company CEOs who've told me they're pleased with their financial results, but their tone was so serious, I couldn't even tell that they were happy. If you've got good news to deliver, make sure you deliver it with enthusiasm!

If you're unsure of what your tone should be, ask yourself how you want people to feel when they are listening to you. Your tone should match how you want them to react.

Pace

When some people get nervous, they tend to talk really fast. The danger of speaking too fast is that inevitably some of the information being shared gets totally lost because the audience just can't keep up. When our mouths work faster than our brains we can either become tongue-tied or say much more than we intended.

What we want to aim for is slowing our pace to a natural, conversational rhythm. Equally, it's important not to go too far in the opposite direction either. If we speak too slowly, we will also lose our audience, perhaps through sheer boredom.

Emphasis

Do you have a keyword in a sentence that you really want to stand out? If that's the case, you need to emphasise it.

Take, for example, the sentence:

> "If there's one thing we want our customers to feel, it is confidence in our product."

Here, you would almost certainly want to put emphasis on the word *confidence*, perhaps by saying it a little louder or with more vocal strength.

Another way you can put emphasis on a particular word, or part of a sentence, is to give the slightest pause just before delivering that word. In this case, it would sound like:

> "If there's one thing we want our customers to feel...[slight pause]...it is confidence in our product".

That slight pause (and it only needs to be ever so slight), will keep your audience hanging on your sentence. Subconsciously, the pause increases their interest in what you're saying, because it breaks the rhythm of the sentence, and the audience waits in anticipation for what is coming next.

Volume

Turn it up! Just a little bit. By increasing our volume ever so slightly in an interview, we can add a significant amount of extra energy to what we're saying. I like to think of this technique as vocal presence. By speaking more loudly, we make our presence felt. A couple of extra decibels can be all it takes to sound like we're speaking with more conviction and authority.

Variety

The key to harnessing the true power of your voice is to embrace variety. Variety means breaking up a monotone, but also not becoming too reliant on any one voice technique alone. You can create variety by varying your tone, pace, sentence length and inflections. A varied voice and delivery gives your key messages stronger impact. As a whole, it makes you a more interesting person to listen to.

Umms and Ahhs

One of the most common questions I get asked in practical media training sessions, is about eliminating umms and ahhs. I always remind people that we all use umms and ahhs as part of our natural, conversational way of talking. They're not something that we need to feel panicked or paranoid about. Problems only arise when they're used too much and distract from our delivery.

Umms and ahhs are what we call verbal filler words. We say them when our brain isn't moving as fast as our mouth and we need to "fill" the space with an empty word. Other filler words that we tend to fall back on include words and phrases such as "like" and "you know".

My first tip for avoiding filler words is to slow your pace down and focus on each individual word you are saying, as you say it. If your delivery is a little slower, your brain will better keep pace with your mouth, and you'll be better able to focus on one word at at a time. When your brain and mouth match each other for pace, there are no gaps to fill, and the umms and ahhs begin to disappear.

My second tip, is to identify where in your sentences you are using filler words. If you're using an umm or an ahh at the beginning of an answer, it means you're filling that air space with an unnecessary sound. Instead, try pausing for a moment or two before answering. Don't be afraid of a tiny bit of silence in this moment. It's OK. If you really need to buy some time to think, try rephrasing the reporter's question in your own words at the start of your answer.

> **PRO TIP : An exercise for umms and ahhs**
>
> Choose an object, a thing or place. It might be an inanimate object in the room you're in, such as a coffee cup. It might be a place you've been on holiday, like Bali. It might be a food, like ice-cream. Your task is to set a stopwatch and record yourself talking about your chosen topic for two minutes. The rule for this exercise is no filler words are allowed! No

> umms, ahhs, you-knows or likes. The trick is to slow your delivery down and think more deliberately about what you want to say. Listen back to yourself and count the umms and ahhs, and spot where in your delivery they are appearing. Try this over and over again, and you will gradually start to notice where you are using filler words, and how slowing your delivery can help you eliminate them.

Your Body

Body language plays a crucial role in communicating any message. Our posture needs to be open, our hands should never be in our pockets, and our arms never folded in front of us.

Posture

In some interviews you'll be seated, for others you'll be standing. In any event, consider what your posture says about you. Hunched shoulders certainly don't project confidence, but leaning all the way back in your chair projects the complete opposite: ego. The key, as in all things, is maintaining balance.

If you're standing, keep your feet planted on the floor about shoulder-width apart. It may help you to have one foot slightly in front of the other so that you can't rock from side-to-side or sway. This way your weight will be balanced.

If you're seated, be careful not to slump forward. If there's a desk, avoid leaning on it. Sit up straight with your hands resting lightly on the desk.

In any interview scenario, also be careful of swivelling chairs. We all have a tendency to move a little bit, and if you're not careful you will be swinging all over the place, which can be very distracting for the audience.

Hands

Many people have a tendency to overthink what they do with their hands. The truth is, we all use our hands to accentuate our conversations, and moving them a little during interviews is no problem. The key is to keep movements small, natural and non-repetitive. Your hands shouldn't move too high (not above your rib cage and certainly not covering your face), nor too wide either. One reason that watching back video recordings of your interviews is helpful is that you will get a good sense of whether your hand movements are problematic or not. For the vast majority of interviewees, they aren't.

In many interviews, even if you're moving your hands, they may well be out of frame of the camera anyway. If wild hand movements are a problem for you, consider holding your hands together in front of you, slightly squeezing the soft skin between your thumb and forefinger with the thumb and forefinger of your other hand. The audience won't notice it, but the slight squeezing will discourage you from moving your hands.

Your Face

Eye contact

Eye contact is crucial in interviews. If your interview is in person, you should always keep eye contact with the reporter. If your eyes wander up, down or to the side, it can make you come across as deceptive, uncertain or lacking confidence. Lock eyes with the reporter or focus on the bridge of their nose. If your interview is a remote interview, keep eye contact with the camera the whole time. If you are ever in doubt where to look, check with the reporter or producer beforehand.

Expression

Your facial expressions will vary with the tone and context of every interview, but as a general rule, you should aim for a warm and friendly expression on your face. I find one of the biggest mistakes that interviewees make is wearing their concentration (or fear!) all over their face. Many of us frown or furrow our brows when we're concentrating on a question or just listening. You will need to consciously focus on warmer facial expressions, so that you project confidence and approachability to the audience throughout your interview.

Smile

Our facial expressions always need to match the tone of an interview, and this is especially the case when you're delivering good news. If your interview is a positive one, a warm, confident smile is a must. You'll find when you have a smile on your face, your tone of voice will match it. After all, if you want the audience smiling at your news, you ought to set an example.

13.

CREATING CALM AND DEALING WITH NERVES

The power of zen

Earlier in the book, I noted that being calm and composed were traits common to all good spokespeople. Maintaining calm is a life skill that is incredibly valuable, well beyond the realm of media interviews. People who are able to remain calm during interviews are generally people who are able to find calm in the many other stressful parts of their lives. Some of the secrets to creating calm, both in everyday life and in interview scenarios are deceptively simple. They require practice though, and discipline too. Becoming a calm person actually takes work, but it is worth the effort.

Embrace your nerves

There's nothing wrong with being a little bit nervous before a big event. Nerves are a natural part of the body's fight or flight responses to stresses and threats. I find the best way to deal with nerves is to change the way we think about them. Rather than trying to fight them off, it can help to acknowledge your nerves, accept that they might make you feel uncomfortable for a short time, but think of them as a reminder that you are about to perform an important task.

Your nerves aren't a warning sign that you're going to fail, they're just a warning sign that what you're doing is important. They're actually there to help you. They let you know that you need to take the situation seriously, and be adequately prepared. They're a reminder that you need to take the job seriously. Once you start thinking about being nervous in this way, you'll find that nerves can become your friend.

Practice. Then practice again. And then some more

The first time any of us rode a bike, we probably fell off. Maybe the second time too. We might have wanted to give up, but sooner or later we got the hang of it. The same is true of interviews. The more you practice them, the better you will become. Make the time to practice mock scenario interviews with your communications team or consultant. Most importantly, record these interviews on video and watch them back, critiquing your performance. Do it again and again. Soon the task of answering questions, especially the difficult ones, will become second nature to you and your confidence will soar.

Anticipate the hard questions

One of the biggest sources of anxiety before an interview

is the fear of the unknown, in particular not knowing what questions the reporter will ask. But you will make your life a lot easier if you spend some time anticipating the questions they might ask and giving thought to the key messages you will bounce to if any of those tricky subjects comes up. Again, practice and rehearse responses to these difficult questions with a member of your communications team or consultant.

Visualise a successful performance

When we think about an event that is causing us some worry or concern, many of us will dwell on all the things that could possibly go wrong and play negative versions of this in our heads ahead of time. We assume the worst will happen, that we'll struggle over words or make mistakes. We're effectively playing a mental movie all about failure in our heads.

These negative thoughts are unhelpful and we need to replace them. We need to play a different movie in our minds. We need to pick up the remote control and play a movie about success in our heads instead of one about failure.

To do so, we need to visualise what every aspect of a successful performance will look and feel like. Sit quietly in a chair and close your eyes. Visualise yourself confidently standing in front of the camera. Visualise the reporter nodding in agreement as you deliver your key messages. Visualise yourself appearing on television. Visualise a later conversation where colleagues tell you what a great job you did. Think about how great this success will make you feel. Devote your mind's energy to focusing on positive visualisations of success rather than unhelpful and unfounded assumptions of failure.

Throw away the mental movie of failure. And keep watching the mental movie of success.

The reporter isn't usually your enemy

I have no doubt that, overwhelmingly, you will find most reporters to be warm, friendly, approachable and helpful. Very few will ever be trying to catch you out, interrogate or investigate you. With this in mind, you can approach your dealings with reporters with confidence. Many of them will even help you to shape your responses in a way that best helps them tell your story. On the whole, reporters want and need your help to make their story succeed. They'll support you to deliver good responses, because your success is their success.

Make life easier with a cheat sheet

You don't have to make things harder for yourself than they need to be. Remember, if your interview is over the telephone (for example, for radio or with an online reporter), you can have a page of notes in front of you. Make sure your key messages and news grabs are in very large print. If there are any key statistics, make sure these are written down. Instead of long sentences and too much detail, perhaps just use buzz words to remind you of your key messages. If you become stuck, you can glance down at your cheat sheet for a reminder. Only use your cheat sheet for help if you need it. If you rely too much on reading from notes, it will be obvious to the interviewer and the audience.

If your interview is in person, you obviously won't be able to have a cheat sheet with you during the interview. But if you're nervous, I still encourage you to make one up to use while you practice. Perhaps even transfer it to a small card for your pocket, so you can study it right up until when you give your interview.

Arrive early

Always give yourself plenty of time to arrive for an in-person interview. There's no more certain way to become more nervous and more flustered than being stuck in traffic on the way to an interview, or worse, missing it altogether because you didn't allow yourself enough time. If you arrive a few minutes early you will have a chance to gather your thoughts and calmly do last-minute preparation.

Perfect is the enemy of good

None of us is perfect, and in interviews especially, we shouldn't try to be. Don't be too hard on yourself for not getting your key messages word perfect when you deliver them. It's the essence that counts. You will sound much more relaxed and come across as a more warm and humble communicator if you focus on being good rather than being perfect. Perfectionists second guess themselves and correct themselves on the fly because they are anxious about being caught out. As a result their communication suffers and they don't effectively deliver their key messages. No one's perfect. Focus on being good.

Make way for meditation

It's difficult to create calm in an instant, just before an interview. A better course of action is to embrace calmness in other aspects of life as a whole. If you are the type of person to become easily stressed or frazzled (and who among us isn't?), it may be worth introducing the practice of meditation into your daily life. Don't have time for it? The people who say that are probably the people who need it the most! There are some helpful apps available for smartphones that can help you even if you've never tried meditation before. Like anything worthwhile, it can be difficult to begin with and requires discipline, but the rewards are life-changing.

Strategies for faster calm

> *PRO TIP: A breathing exercise*
>
> Working on our breathing can help not just our nerves, but also our voice and delivery. When we are stressed, our breathing rate increases, just like our heart rate. When we're taking more breaths, our words become stilted, and our sentences more broken up. We gasp for air at the end of a sentence or take a big deep breath in the middle of it. Taking

control of our breathing can improve every aspect of our performance.

Before an interview, or at any time really, taking big, long, deep breaths can help get you back in control.

First, breathe all of the air that you can get out of your lungs. Do it nice and slowly, but get it all out. Out, out, out!

Then, inhale, slowly until your lungs are completely full. Hold your breath for as long as you comfortably can. Then let it out.

Repeat. Then repeat again for a total of 10 times.

The whole exercise should only take you a couple of minutes, but you will have slowed your heart rate down and introduced some regularity to your breathing, and a new sense of calm to your disposition. This is handy for use not just before interviews, but any time that you need to restore a sense of calm.

PRO TIP: *Relax your muscles*

Find a comfortable chair and shut your eyes. You're going to relax your entire body, one section at a time, from your top to your toes by clenching and then relaxing the muscles.

Focus on your face first. Your eyes, your nose, your mouth. Moving down your body, spend 10-20 seconds at each stop, relaxing that muscle group.

After your head, trace this relaxing movement down. Your neck is next, and then your shoulders. Then your chest, lower back and down your arms. Next your backside, your legs from top to bottom and finally your toes.

Repeat this exercise in the opposite direction, going up your body instead. At the end, your heart rate will have slowed, your body will have relaxed, and your mind will have been given the opportunity to reset.

14.

QUESTIONS I ALWAYS GET ASKED

How often should I repeat my key messages in an interview?

More than once! When competing for people's attention, a message is more likely to be remembered by your audience and make an impact on them if it is repeated. It's how advertising works too: when we hear something often enough, it begins to stick in our memory. But please allow for a little nuance here. While some repetition of our key messages is a good thing, there's a sweet spot between making your message stick, and it becoming tiresome or boring to the interviewer and audience if repeated ad-nauseum, with no other insights. This is the reason that I encourage you to have several key messages based around your broad goal for the interview. This way you can continually weave a different message into your responses, while avoiding sounding boring or repetitive.

Am I allowed to see a story before it is published or broadcast?

You wish! Once you've done your interview, the story is in the reporter's hands. It can be daunting to have to wait and see what the story looks like and which quotes of yours they have decided to use, but nothing will get you more offside with a reporter than asking to check their work. Remember, this is why it is so important to give a strong performance in your interview in the first place and also why you need to be circumspect about everything that you say to the reporter.

What if I'm taken out of context?

I'll be honest. There are some unethical reporters out there who might twist or manipulate your words. But my experience is that those reporters are very much in the minority. When someone claims to have been misquoted, sometimes they're right. But frequently, the reason that they might feel they have been misquoted, is that they weren't clear in their communication during the interview in the first place. This is also a poignant reminder about the importance of being cautious when interviews stray into difficult topic areas. Remember, the less you say about problematic issues, the less you can be quoted on. If there is something that you want to make absolutely clear in an interview, preface it with some signalling language prior to delivering the message. Some signalling language could be:

- "Let me make this crystal clear..."
- "Just so there's no confusion..."

- "I can't be any clearer about this…"
- "Let me repeat this again…"

What if I just don't think it's a story?

It's a story if it's in the newspaper. It's a story if it's on television. In fact, an issue is becoming a story the moment a reporter starts sniffing around about it. You mightn't think the issue warrants attention, but telling a reporter that isn't going to make it go away. You need to deal with reality and understand that the earlier you respond, the better chance you have to shape the outcome of a story. It's at these times that having an experienced communications team or consultant to help you is particularly worthwhile.

Why can't I just say "no comment" and move on?

You can, if you want to look guilty and evasive. Of course, there will be times you really can't comment on a particular issue, perhaps for legal, commercial or privacy reasons. But even in these circumstances, you shouldn't use the words "no comment".

There's always something you can say, even if it's not directly about the issue on which the reporter is questioning you. This means using a bounce phrase to get away from the part of the question you can't answer, and toward a message that you are comfortable delivering.

For example, if asked:

> *"Are you worried about the court case?"*

One way to deal with this question would be to say:

> *"Look, that matter is still before the courts, so legally there's very little I can say. What I will say though, more broadly, is that we're getting on with the job of rebuilding the company and…"*

Journalists will know that there are certain issues you aren't allowed to comment on, but this doesn't mean they won't try asking about them. They might even ask several times. It's their job to give it a try, it's your job to hold your ground.

Can I walk out of an interview if the reporter is being a jerk?

This is a very bad idea. Sure, you might be uncomfortable with the questioning, but if you walk out, you can almost guarantee that the reporter will use the footage of you storming out of the interview to promote the story and characterise you as unstable or untrustworthy. Unless you're a wild rock star trying to court controversy on purpose, then it's not a good idea. Some politicians have tried the storm-off technique too, but I'm yet to see it improve their standing in the community or chances of re-election. If you're not happy with a line of questioning, you should use the bounce technique to return to your key messages. Remember, you don't have to like the reporter or even get along with them, but your tone and manner tells the audience as much as your words do, and sometimes even more. An audience is likely to judge you harshly if you show aggression.

Can I give some comments "off the record"?

You should consider that everything you say to a reporter, in any context — on the phone, by email, in a bar, over coffee, anywhere really — might be quoted in a story. You have to be cautious in your dealings with reporters. Even if you've known them for years, you should remember that at times, their professional goals and objectives will be different to yours.

You might have heard the phrases "off the record" or "on background". This is where you talk to the reporter on condition of anonymity. If I were you, I'd leave this tactic to people who have many years experience of dealing with journalists. If you feel you really need to give a reporter some information that you don't want attributed to you, ask your communications team or consultant for advice.

What happens if I stuff up?

Learn from it. If you make a mistake, try to understand why it happened and don't let it stop you from giving another interview in the future. Some of our most well recognised politicians, sports stars, entertainers and corporate leaders have made mistakes in interviews. We all have bad days. The most important thing is how we learn from them.

Besides, are you sure you genuinely stuffed up? Or are you being a little harsh on yourself? We can often be our own worst critics when it comes to our own performance. Check in with colleagues and ask their opinion of how it went. Their view might be different to yours.

Can I make my own recording of an interview?

You can, and sometimes it's a good idea, but you don't want to create any unnecessary tension in the interview with the reporter by doing so. Some people like to make their own recordings so they can correct the record if any of their remarks are taken out of context, or perhaps you might want to review the recording to improve your performance in the future. If you do want to make your own recording, you must let the other party know. Just be aware that the reporter might interpret this as a sign that you don't trust them. This could affect your relationship with them and the way they frame the story, so think about whether you really need to do it.

What about one-word answers. Are they OK?

No. (See what I did there?) Why would you give a one-word answer when you have fabulous, well thought-out key messages to deliver? I know I've encouraged you to be concise in your responses to difficult questions, but one-word answers make you sound evasive and possibly rude. Even if the answer to a question is a simple yes or no, there is always more you can add by using a bounce statement and then elaborating on one of your key messages.

Should I call reporters by name in an interview?

I'd avoid it. It might feel like you're making a warm connection with them, but this might come at the expense of your connection with the audience. Remember, you're talking to the audience, not just the interviewer. Also, if the interview is pre-recorded rather than live, it can render some of your sound bites useless if you've jammed the reporter's name in the middle of them.

Should I thank them for having me on the program at the start of the interview?

Politely thanking people is a sign of good manners in other parts of life, but it's not really necessary at the start of an interview. Some people start an interview by effusively thanking the host for the opportunity to be there, and although it might seem polite, it's a waste of valuable interview time. Just get on with your response and get to the point. It will be obvious from your presence on the program and your tone in answering that you are delighted and grateful to be there. Being warm and cordial throughout the whole interview is a better way to impress the audience than heaping gratitude on the host at the start.

There's so much I want to say about a topic, I can't possibly condense it all down. What do I do?

Your time in an interview is limited, so being brief and concise with your answers is key. But if there is more information that you think the audience should know, feel free to direct them to your website or helpline number and explain that there is more information there. And don't just say "our website has more information", tell the audience the exact address. Make life easier for them.

Why is there a different reporter's name on the story to the one who actually interviewed me?

Teamwork on their part, mostly. Sometimes stories are written as a team effort by a group of reporters. A story might be started by one reporter, but they might later get assigned a different task and pass their work on to a colleague to complete. In television, sometimes you'll find a producer will interview you instead of a reporter. They work as a team because sometimes it's not possible for the reporter to be present for the interview. This is another reason not to use the reporter's name in your responses!

Should I use acronyms or jargon?

It's best if you can avoid them, but it really depends on whether a typical member of the audience will understand them or not. My advice is that if you absolutely have to use jargon, acronyms or highly technical terms, then you should very briefly define them, at their first use.

Here's how that could work in practice:

> *"The best part of the NDIS – that's the National Disability Insurance Scheme – is that it helps us to implement..."*

From then on, you could continue using the acronym NDIS. A rule of thumb is that if you can't explain a term in just a few words, you should avoid it.

What about promises that are hard to keep?

It's important to excite and engage your audience, but it's also crucial that you don't make promises or guarantees you can't keep, or that could be used against you in the future. Language matters, so choose your words carefully. Don't oversell if you can't deliver.

So instead of:

> "The new treatments will cure the cancer."

You could try:

> "Success in trials so far has filled me with confidence."

And instead of:

> "We will never have another safety incident at this school."

You could try:

> "We're committed to always providing a safe environment for students."

Why do an interview? Why not just issue a statement?

Especially in times of crisis, some organisations will choose to issue a statement rather than have an executive interviewed. The thinking is that they'll escape some of the negative attention and avoid making it worse by potentially misspeaking in an interview. It's important to think carefully about this and take advice from your communications team or consultant. By issuing statements rather than consenting to interviews, you may appear evasive and give the impression that you have something to hide.

Can I learn from others?

Yes. I really encourage you to become a more active consumer of media if you're going to be a participant in it. Start watching interviews through a new prism. Note the questions that are asked and what you like or don't like about the answers. Start to notice what makes some interviewees more memorable, and the sound bites they use or the tone they take. If the interviewee is from your industry, even better. Put yourself in their shoes and think of how you'd have handled the questions, especially the difficult ones.

Can I stop a story from running?

If you know a story that will affect your reputation is coming, I can understand the desire to do what's possible to stop it. Sometimes there are legal reasons to put a stop to a story, and in these cases individuals or organisations can go to court to seek an injunction to restrict or delay publication or broadcast. Just remember that your actions in taking this legal action might also be reported, and doing so could make an already bad situation even worse. It's an area where you should tread carefully and seek out the best possible advice from your legal advisors and communications team.

I want to sue them! Can I?

Individuals can sue for defamation of character, and some small businesses can too. The media certainly don't always get it right, and some of our most well-known and celebrated broadcasters and publications have been successfully sued for defamation, or settled out of court with large payouts. That said, litigation is an expensive and stressful process that you ought to think carefully about before commencing.

Will the reporter give me a list of their questions?

As a reporter, I never liked it when an interview subject or public relations minder asked for a list of questions before an interview. Such a request always meant the interview got off on the wrong foot. This was for a couple of reasons. First, I had a sense of pride in my role as a reporter, and felt my job was to hold all of my interview subjects to account. Letting them sticky-beak at questions meant I wasn't doing my job properly. But you know what else? Most times, I wouldn't come to an interview with a list of questions, especially when I became a more experienced reporter. I'd come with an open mind and allow the interview to flow naturally. I'd listen carefully, and sometimes the answers an interviewee gave would totally change the course of the interview. All of that said, there's no harm in asking the general topics the reporter wants to cover. But even if you were given a list of questions, it could provide a false sense of security. There's no guarantee the reporter wouldn't diverge from them. Part of your preparation should be to get ready for all sorts of questions that may arise.

When does the interview start and end?

In the movies, the reporter puts the tape recorder on the desk and hits record, and the interview starts, or the camera operator yells "I'm rolling", and the inquisition is under way. But the truth is that every interaction you have with a reporter, including your emails, general chit-chat and small talk before and after the interview, your text messages, and in fact anything else can be quoted and used as part of the story.

For broadcast interviews, you need to be especially careful about everything you say. Even when you're not filming your actual interview and even if you're not wearing a microphone, the camera might still be on and recording. Internal camera microphones and boom microphones can pick up audio too.

I'm not saying you ought to be paranoid. My earlier advice that reporters generally aren't out to get you rings true in almost every case. But just be on your guard, and never say anything you wouldn't want to end up seeing on TV or reading in print.

PART II

MEDIA TRAINING: WHAT THEY SHOULD HAVE KNOWN

15.

REAL WORLD MEDIA TRAINING LESSONS

In media interviews as in life, it's always a good idea to learn from our mistakes. But it's even easier, and a lot less painful, to learn lessons from the mistakes of others instead. Below you'll find a collection of my favourite tales from media interviews gone wrong, around Australia and the world. From politicians to princes, sporting legends to celebrities, and executives to entrepreneurs, this is your chance to learn a lesson and avoid making the mistakes that they did.

Aussie politicians and dangerous backdrops

The tale

Politicians have a team of assistants whose job it is to ensure that the leader is never filmed, photographed or interviewed in front of a backdrop that could somehow distract from their message. The assistants are known as "advancers", and they travel to the interview location before the politician and the rest of the entourage arrive to make sure that the location is suitable, and nothing about the environment will cause a distraction. But even the best laid plans can go awry.

In 2015, then Australian prime minister Tony Abbott found himself filmed and photographed in front of The Reject Shop, a retail store in a Canberra shopping precinct, well known for its bargains. A media event had been planned for a butcher shop nearby, but for photographers, jagging images of the the prime minister with the adjacent discount store in the background proved an irresistible temptation.

Leaders on both side of politics have suffered embarrassment as a result of backdrops or environments that reflected poorly on their messaging. In 2013, former prime minister Kevin Rudd was speaking to a group of students at a high school where the walls of the history classroom featured prominent photographs of Adolf Hitler and Benito Mussolini. It's fair to say that most politicians would prefer not to be pictured in the same frame as these figures from history.

The lesson

It's not just what you say and how you say it. Backdrop and location are crucial, and to the extent that you can control the environment of your interview, you should. Anything that may distract from your message or potentially embarrass you should be avoided at all costs. This is true whether you are holding a press conference in public, a TV crew is coming to visit, or you're being interviewed via Zoom from your lounge room.

The empty chair at ABC's 7.30

The tale

If you think you can get away with refusing interviews forever without any consequences, you should think again. You could become a victim of an empty chair interview! One politician who learnt this the hard way in 2020 was former sports minister Bridget McKenzie on ABC's 7.30. The context was that McKenzie was continually refusing the program's requests for an interview to address public criticism and concern over a controversial sports funding program. But when requests for an interview were continually rebuffed, the program found a creative way to let its audience know that the minister was being evasive. After airing a taped segment about the issue, the broadcast flashed to a shot of an empty chair, where a guest would usually be seated for interview.

The program's host, Leigh Sales, then started asking questions of the empty chair, as if the politician was there. "Here's what we'd ask her on behalf of the Australian public," she said, before continuing with an extensive list of questions.

The lesson

This tale is a reminder that refusing to be interviewed about a story is no guarantee that the story will go away. It demonstrates that there are times when your ongoing refusal to answer questions could be shared with readers and viewers, reflecting poorly on you. Even though your intention might be to stay out of the story, a technique like the empty chair interview shows that this could backfire, and make a bad situation worse.

Barack Obama's chit-chat

The tale

Political leaders are among the most experienced at handling media interviews, but that doesn't mean they don't make mistakes. In 2009, a TV news crew was setting up for an interview with US president Barack Obama. While the equipment was still being set up and the interview hadn't technically started yet, there was some general chit-chat between crew and the president. They were talking about a recent incident where Kanye West had stormed the stage while Taylor Swift was collecting an award at the MTV Video awards.

"What's he doing up there? He's a jackass!" Obama said. If you watch the video, you can see the president seemed to realise immediately that his of-the-cuff remarks might have been recorded by one of the cameras. "Come on guys, cut the president some slack," he implored.

But they didn't. The tape was leaked. And the "jackass" comment spread across the internet. While Obama may not have suffered long-term damage from the gaffe, it shows how easily these lapses of judgment can happen.

The lesson

A lot can happen on the set of a recorded interview before the questions begin. Camera operators are busy setting up cameras and adjusting lights. Make-up artists might be performing touch-ups to the interviewer or interviewee. It's a distracting environment where it's easy to let your guard down, especially when you want to be personable and polite to anyone who is present. The lesson for all interviewees is to be abundantly careful about cameras and microphones, even when the interview hasn't officially started, or even when you think it has officially finished. Assume the cameras are always rolling.

Caught off guard by a boom microphone

The tale

Microphones come in many shapes and forms. Some will be lapel microphones, attached to your clothing. But you don't have to be wearing a clipped-on lapel microphone for what you're saying to be recorded. Powerful boom microphones are incredibly sensitive and can capture audio from some distance away. Many politicians and others have discovered just how powerful the microphones are, getting caught out saying something that they'd rather not have been made public at a time when they thought they wouldn't be heard.

In 2015, then immigration minister Peter Dutton was taking part in a photo opportunity with prime minister Tony Abbott and social services minister Scott Morrison. Dutton was quipping to his colleagues that "time doesn't mean anything when you're about to have water lapping at your door". This was perceived as an insensitive reference to the effects of climate change on rising sea levels for Pacific Island nations. Alert to the risk of the remarks being captured on camera, Morrison pointed quietly to a boom microphone and said "there's a boom up there", with Abbott adding "yeah, yeah".

The recording went public, and Dutton was criticised. He later apologised saying he "should have realised the mic was there and didn't".

He wasn't the first and won't be the last to be caught out by the power of a boom microphone. In 2005, Prince Charles found himself the subject of criticism after he was caught out during a photo opportunity in the ski fields with Prince William and Prince Harry. Seemingly unaware that his voice was being recorded while photos were being taken, he was caught off guard talking to his sons about one of the reporters. "Bloody people. I can't bear that man. He's so awful. He really is," he was recorded saying. Prince Charles didn't have a great relationship with the press at the time, and the gaffe did nothing to improve that.

The lesson

Just because you aren't wearing a microphone or you can't see one, doesn't mean that sound isn't being recorded. You ought to be on guard at all times, even if the chance of being recorded feels unlikely. An ill-judged remark, intended or not, can damage a reputation, sometimes irreparably.

Upsetting the Wolf of Wall Street

The tale

When Liz Hayes interviewed Jordon Belfort, the so-called "Wolf of Wall Street" for Australia's 60 Minutes in 2014, the interview quickly turned sour when she began asking questions about the former stockbroker's personal finances. Belfort didn't like the questions and in a moment of drama, he got up and started to storm out of the interview. Here's how the altercation was presented in the story.

> Belfort:
> "Next question. [At this point he stands up and walks out of the interview] I think you can air what you want to air out of this interview, it's done."
>
> Reporter:
> "Why can't I a...?"
>
> Belfort (off camera):
> "....Oh my god, you've got a lot of nerve boy, I tell you! Honest, really."
>
> Reporter:
> "Why can't I ask these questions?"
>
> Belfort:
> "I was told this was a friendly, nice interview and no one has ever treated me as disrespectfully as you have."

The lesson

There are two lessons for interviewees here. The first is to understand and anticipate that you might be asked questions you don't like, even if you believe you have an agreement with the reporter that the interview will be friendly. Your job is to think in advance how you'll respond if such questions arise. The second lesson is that storming out of an interview only gives tabloid television programs more fodder for their stories. The only time that storming out of an interview is a good idea is if you actually want the sort of publicity that comes with it. For some individuals (perhaps Belfort might be one of them) the bold action matches their personal brand and will endear them to their supporters. But for most, it's not a good look.

Ronald Reagan's dangerous sarcasm

The tale

In 1984, president Ronald Reagan was recording a scheduled radio address about high schools. In the days before cable television and online news, pre-recorded radio addresses were often used as a way for the president to keep in touch with the general public.

But before recording the actual address, Reagan was joking with technicians about Russia. He sarcastically said, "My fellow Americans, I'm pleased to tell you that today I've signed legislation that will outlaw Russia forever. We begin bombing in five minutes." The problem was that the remarks had been recorded, and distributed unintentionally to some radio stations around the country. Yikes!

Reporting of the remarks did nothing to help tensions between the United States and Soviet Union at the time, and Reagan's poll numbers also took a hit as a result of the gaffe.

The lesson

Joking around, being sarcastic and saying things you don't really mean, are rarely a good idea both during an interview, and at any time you are talking to a reporter or near recording equipment. You just never know where the recording might end up. In the wrong context, it's very easy for sarcasm or other jokes to be misinterpreted and cause a lot of damage.

An Aussie politician forgets his messages

The tale

In 2013, an aspiring politician for the Liberal Party, Jaymes Diaz, was campaigning in Western Sydney and was interviewed by a journalist about his party's well-publicised six-point plan for dealing with asylum seekers attempting to reach Australia.

But when Network Ten reporter John Hill asked the reasonable question "the six points, could you run through them for us?", the political candidate was unable to do so. What followed was an excruciating six-minute interview where the television reporter persisted with asking the candidate to spell out the six points, which he couldn't.

The interview went viral and the candidate was ultimately unsuccessful in his bid to win the seat. It was one of the most memorable moments of the 2013 election campaign.

The lesson

The lesson for all interviewees is the value and importance of preparation. In this case, if the six-point plan was a cornerstone of a political campaign, it was crucial that all candidates were able to recite the points. If data, statistics or key messages are important, then they must be etched into your memory. But if you do get caught out and can't recall particular information on the spot, it might be better to acknowledge your momentary memory lapse rather than fumble through it.

Nick Kyrgios' unique interview style

The tale

Tennis players, like many sportspeople, are compelled to participate in press conferences after matches during major tournaments. Australian player Nick Kyrgios is an example of one player well known for some of his exchanges with reporters, including this one from Wimbledon in 2015.

> Reporter:
> "You didn't return the serves. It looked like you weren't trying, which is very unusual at Wimbledon."
>
> Kyrgios:
> "Do you want to try to return Richard Gasquet's serve?

> I'll give you the racket and we'll see how many times you can return his serve."

Reporter:
"You're a professional player. I'm not."

Kyrgios' candid style was polarising. Some people loved his directness. Others may have found it a little rude. The thing is, for sportspeople and entertainers, a polarising style can sometimes really work for them, contributing to the growth of their personal brand and identity. For others though, in business or politics, turning questions back on the reporter is a tactic that usually backfires.

The lesson

What works for Nick Kyrgios and other sports stars and entertainers may not work for you. If you try the tactic of putting the reporter on trial, an audience is likely to judge you critically. Interactions with journalists shouldn't be treated as contests to be won or lost, and reporters as adversaries to be defeated. And when you pick a fight with a reporter, you are wasting valuable interview time that would be better spent trying to get your key messages across.

What happened to Kourtney?

The tale

When Kourtney Kardashian was a live satellite guest on Today Extra in October 2016, her publicity team might have hoped that all the questions would be about the new skincare range that she was promoting. But earlier in the month, her sister Kim had been the victim of a terrifying robbery in Paris. The hosts recognised that their audience would be interested in knowing how Kim was recovering, and so asked some questions about it. But instead of either answering the question, or trying to deflect to another topic, Kourtney's response took a strange turn.

> Host:
> "We were wondering, how is everyone going and how is Kim doing?"
>
> Kourtney:
> "Umm… [looking off camera and talking to someone else] *Okay.*"
>
> Host:
> "I'm sorry is there someone talking to you?"
>
> Kourtney:
> "Yeah sorry, they just came in."

Oddly, what is understood to have happened, is that an assistant, unhappy with the line of questioning, had come into the studio mid-interview and interrupted off-camera when the question about the robbery was asked.

At the awkward moment, the interview was paused, and when Kourtney returned after the break, she happily talked about the robbery issue, as well as the product she was on the program to promote.

The lesson

When you're on live TV, you're on your own, and shouldn't receive any input from your team or advisors. The lesson here is as much for communications advisors as it is for interviewees: once the interview is underway, the advisors should leave you to it, even if they're unhappy with the line of questioning. Interviewees should be empowered to judge which questions they ought to engage with and should be well versed in tactics such as the bounce technique to move conversations to areas they'd prefer to talk about. In this case, it should have been assumed that the interviewers would ask about about the robbery. You should always expect a good interviewer to acknowledge the elephant in the room. That's their job.

Prince Andrew's right royal mess

The tale

In 2019, Prince Andrew gave an interview to the BBC's Emily Maitlis to address issues relating to his friendship with convicted sex offender Jeffrey Epstein. His performance was widely derided.

Some questioned whether he should have participated in the interview at all, given how poorly it was handled. If its intent was to provide explanations, or rehabilitate his image, it failed. In one instance, when talking about regretting a decision to stay at Epstein's home, Prince Andrew said that he had "let the side down". The side he is referring to is the royal family and using the language of a football game to describe a response to abuse was very poor judgment.

In another moment in the interview, Prince Andrew described Epstein as having behaved "in a manner unbecoming". When the interviewer challenged this, saying, "unbecoming? He was a sex offender!" she had the same astonished reaction as anyone watching would have.

Much of the criticism of these moments and others in the interview was centred on the Prince appearing tone-deaf to the gravity of the situation and the impact it had on victims.

The lesson

It's a little difficult knowing where to start on the many lessons learnt here. This interview is a lesson in the importance of tone, and understanding audience perception. At the outset, the Prince should have been cognisant of the fact that the subject matter related to a situation where victims of a horrific crime were undergoing immense pain. The tone of the interview ought to have been empathetic, compassionate and understanding. The old advice to "read the room" is valid here.

Big oil boss makes a big mistake

The tale

One of the biggest international stories of 2010 involved petroleum company BP. An oil spill, which caused an environmental catastrophe and killed 11 people, had the company in the headlines for all the wrong reasons. But if you thought the situation couldn't get worse, it did.

At a press conference, the company's CEO made an astonishing gaffe, telling reporters, "There's no one who wants this over more than I do, I'd like my life back." Anger in the community was palpable and he later apologised for the comments. But that was generally regarded as too little, too late. The PR situation was made even worse when another executive said "we care about the small people".

The lesson

It's not about you. In a catastrophe or crisis, any impact or inconvenience to you is insignificant compared to the impact on victims. Words and tone really matter. Very few people will feel empathy for a well-paid corporate executive complaining during a crisis. One of the reasons that leaders are well paid is because of the expectation they may have to handle crises such as these. Do your job and don't complain about it.

A motoring enthusiast joins the Senate

The tale

In 2014, thanks to a peculiarity of our electoral system, a number of politicians with very little experience were elected to the Australian Senate representing minor parties. Among them was Ricky Muir from the Motoring Enthusiast Party. When interviewed by veteran broadcaster Mike Willesee, Muir learnt how excruciating a grilling from an experienced journalist can be.

"Muir fumbles his way through rare media interview", screamed one headline in The Sydney Morning Herald. "Ricky Muir stumbles through interview on Senate role," reported The Guardian. How did he stumble? Among other gaffes, he was unable to answer fairly straightforward questions about policy areas relating to car manufacturing. Muir trailed off in a rambling response before asking "sorry can we start that question again?". His second attempt led him to again trail off once more, saying, "um sorry can we go to another question? I've got myself into a fluster." The program also aired an attempt by Muir to take a break from the interview, saying "can I go out for a minute?"

It was agonising to watch.

The lesson

Don't expect interviewers to go easy on you just because you are new to the game. Even if you are on training wheels, if you're in a key role of responsibility, you can't expect to be treated with kid gloves, especially when being interviewed by one of the nation's best. It's important to be adequately prepared. The repercussions of a bad interview can be felt long after it's over.

John Hewson's birthday cake

The tale

Ten days before the 1993 election, then opposition leader John Hewson was interviewed on A Current Affair about tax reform policies, including a mooted GST. At the time, there were questions about how the proposed tax would be applied to different items including food, and renowned interviewer Mike Willesee used an example of a birthday cake, to try to better understand Hewson's policy.

> Interviewer:
> "If I buy a birthday cake from a cake shop and GST is in place, do I pay more or less for that birthday cake?"
>
> Hewson:
> "...If it is a cake shop, a cake from a cake shop that has sales tax, and it's decorated and has candles as you say, that attracts sales tax, then of course we scrap the sales tax, before the GST is..."
>
> Willesee:
> "OK — it's just an example. If the answer to a birthday cake is so complex — you do have a problem with the overall GST?"

Hewson's inability to give a simple answer to a simple question about a birthday cake demonstrated how confusing his policy was to voters. The interview became a turning point in the election campaign, which Hewson's party lost later that month.

The lesson

If you have complex information or complicated policy, you absolutely must rehearse a simple way to explain it so people will understand. If viewers or readers don't understand what you are saying, it's almost impossible to win them over. Talented interviewers will act as advocates for their audience, and if they think what you're saying is confusing or doesn't make sense, they'll call you out on it. Be ready with simple explanations for complex concepts. If you aren't ready, like Mr Hewson, you will have "a problem".

Rolls Royce CEO

The tale

In May 2020, the CEO of Rolls Royce was being interviewed on the BBC via webcam about reports of thousands of job losses at the company. It became apparent that the CEO was distracted by someone or something, off-camera, while being questioned and he lost his composure. He appeared to be smirking while the interviewer was asking questions about job losses, an emotional topic requiring sensitivity and compassion. He lost eye contact with the camera and lost a connection with the audience in doing so. An audience member may easily have drawn the conclusion that he was arrogant and lacked any empathy for people who could be losing their jobs.

The lesson

Remote interviews via webcam are no less serious than those conducted in the studio. As an interviewee, it's important to make sure that your interview space is distraction free. Firstly, there shouldn't be any distractions for the audience behind you. But also, make sure there isn't anything in front of you that could distract you. This includes friends, family, colleagues and pets. It's easy to lose your composure and concentration if they're there.

Supermarket boss sings "We're in the Money"

The tale

In 2018, the boss of UK chain Sainsbury's needed to apologise to customers after an embarrassing gaffe, when he was recorded singing to himself while waiting to be interviewed by ITV News. The singing was captured by the camera and later made public.

But it wasn't just *that* he was singing, it was *what* he was singing. The company's boss was singing, "We're in the Money", a popular show tune from the musical 42nd Street, but a bad choice when the interview was to be about an upcoming merger that some feared would lead to job losses or store closures.

The boss issued an apology saying it was "an unguarded moment trying to compose myself before TV interview...an unfortunate choice of song...and I apologise if I have offended anyone".

The lesson

Which lesson do we choose here? Don't sing? And if you're going to sing, don't sing *that* song? Most of us, hopefully, wouldn't make the same mistake, but it's a reminder to anyone participating in recorded TV interviews that the camera may be rolling long before the interview actually starts. It's important that once you enter the studio, you take extreme care with everything you say and do. This includes answering phone calls and talking to the people around you.

CHRIS URQUHART'S "EDGE" TRAINING COURSES

Chris Urquhart's "Media Edge" media training courses

As comprehensive as this book is, nothing quite compares to joining me for a highly practical, deeply immersive, in-person media training experience. My "Media Edge" training courses have become the leading choice of CEOs, sportspeople, politicians, entertainers, entrepreneurs and leaders from some of Australia's and the world's best known brands. There are various, training options for "Media Edge", including:

- Half-day courses
- Full-day courses
- Follow-up refreshers
- Bespoke workshops
- Remote online training

The most popular format for "Media Edge" training is a small group session where several leaders from the same organisation participate in training as a team, over a half or full-day session. Each session is individually tailored to the participants in the room and is adapted to their industry, experience, media targets and issues facing their organisation.

The most exciting part of in-person training is the opportunity for participants to be interviewed several times on camera, in realistic TV interview scenarios with a full camera crew present. There's also the chance to take part in radio, podcast, print and online style interviews. For those with advanced requirements, you can even get experience hosting a press conference, reading an autocue, handling a satellite style TV live cross or facing the stress of a tabloid ambush interview.

The courses help you develop and then vocalise your key messages in proactive media interviews but also build confidence to handle difficult questions in reactive interviews or crisis situations. I also help you to generate and deliver the perfect sound bite. The "lights, camera, action" approach helps participants immerse themselves completely in the interview experience and become more comfortable in front of the camera. As part of training, we watch your rehearsal interviews back on the big screen, and I deliver instant feedback so that you can improve with every interview.

"Media Edge" media training course can be adapted for groups of any size and any experience level. I've trained groups of 50+ participants, but typically work with a group of 4-5 leaders from the same organisation at any given time. I recommend that several members of your leadership team attend the course so that everyone can gain an understanding of how the media works. This ensures that not only will you have multiple media spokespeople trained and ready, but that your messaging will be consistent across the team. For busy executives unable to attend in a group setting with their peers, bespoke one-on-one sessions are also possible.

"Media Edge" media training can be delivered at a location that is most convenient for you. We can visit your offices anywhere in Australia or you are welcome to visit our Immediate Communications headquarters in Sydney. If you haven't had the opportunity to take part in practical, in-person, media training, an immersive session is a great next step.

Chris Urquhart's "Confidence Edge" communications courses

While media training is important for executives, it's also important that team members at any level in an organisation gain the skills and confidence to present and speak in front of their peers with warmth, clarity and conviction. The problem is that many people list public speaking as their greatest fear. But it doesn't have to be!

My "Confidence Edge" training courses help individuals at all career levels gain a toolkit of skills to deliver effective presentations and speak confidently in front of other people. Whether it's for speaking at staff meetings, pitching to clients or giving keynotes at conferences, "Confidence Edge" offers strategies to succeed in communications.

The "Confidence Edge" courses help with presentation content and structure and help participants understand the importance of taking the audience on a journey. Central to the course is learning the power of storytelling and the importance of harnessing your voice and tone to speak with warmth, passion, authority and emotion. We cover non-verbal communication, including facial expressions, gestures, body language and movement. We also consider other impact tools, including visual aids.

A range of course options are available for business teams including:

- Multi-session training, where team members develop their own presentation for delivery in the final session
- Full-day intensive training
- One hour workshop and lunch-and-learn sessions

For more training resources and information about booking a course, email contact@immediate.net.au or visit our website:

www.immediate.net.au

ABOUT CHRIS URQUHART

Chris Urquhart is the director of Immediate Communications, a communications training and video storytelling company based in Sydney, Australia. At Immediate Communications, Chris uses his years of experience in the media to help businesses and their teams to tell their stories.

After graduating from the University of Sydney with a Bachelor of Arts (Media and Communications) in 2003, Chris began his media career working in radio, with his first on-air role as a news reporter and newsreader at the Austereo Network's 2DayFM and Triple M. In 2005 he relocated to Brisbane to join Nova 106.9FM as a newsreader. In Brisbane, he also spent time as a newsreader for ABC Online and ABC2 digital, and filed stories for Seven News while also contributing to Sky News.

In 2008, Chris returned to Sydney and took up a role as a reporter at Nine News, joining the network's high profile nightly investigative program, A Current Affair, two years later. In 2014, Chris joined Today, reporting for the popular breakfast program for several years. During this period, from time-to-time, Chris was a backup host on both the

Weekend Today and Mornings programs. Later, Chris filed stories for ABC's 7.30 program and was a regular opinion columnist for news.com.au, before devoting his time and energy to Immediate Communications full-time.

In his "Media Edge" training programs, Chris has trained many hundreds of executives, business leaders, spokespeople and sportspeople in the art of handling journalists and delivering media interviews that make an impact. He's also worked with non-executive staff at all career levels in his "Confidence Edge" programs, which improve general confidence, communications and presentation skills for all members of a business team.

In his role as director of Immediate Communications, Chris is regularly sought out for commentary and analysis by some of Australia's best known media outlets and is frequently asked to moderate and speak at conferences, panel discussions and events.

www.ingramcontent.com/pod-product-compliance
Lightning Source LLC
Chambersburg PA
CBHW051432290426
44109CB00016B/1518